The 47 Laws of Success

A Simple Guide to Your Ideal Life

Henry Bergen

PYP BOOKS

PYP

For my father, the first successful man I ever met.

Contents

A Gift for You

Before you dive into this book, I want to let you know about a FREE gift I have for you. I would like to give you a copy of the Productive Cheatsheet, where you will find my ten top tips that to *double* your productivity TODAY. This simple tool will help you take massive steps toward achieving your most ambitious goals. I guarantee it.

Pick your gift at:
https://planyourpotential.com/cheatsheet/

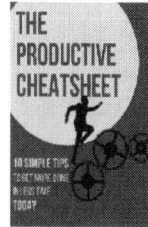

Introduction

Success is the progressive realization of a worthy goal or ideal.

—Earl Nightengale

Success, for most people, is elusive and mysterious: everybody wants it, but only a select few seem to know how to get it. For most of my life, I thought about success like a club that only admits super-geniuses who have made some ground-breaking innovation, or complete buffoons who have accidentally fallen into their good fortune simply by being in the right place at the right time. I assumed that there were two paths to success: the path of the genius or the path of dumb luck. And, because I am not among the 0.03% of the population who have an IQ over 160, nor do I have a closet full of rabbit feet at home, I couldn't see a clear path to success for an average person like me.

But I've since learned that this is a big fat lie—a lie that, unfortunately, a lot of people still believe. I've learned that, in reality, success is just like everything else in the world: it's predictable, *if* you know the laws that govern it. We've all learned in school that the world works according to specific, unchanging, natural laws. We all know about scientific laws, for example, such as the law of gravity or the laws of thermodynamics. Most of us probably also know some basic mathematical laws, such as the law of addition or the law of subtraction. Depending on your background, you might also be familiar with various economic laws, psychological laws, or moral laws. Millions of natural laws exist that describe the way things are in various domains of life. We've learned them over centuries of trial and error, and they're important today because they help us understand how our world works and how we can operate in it.

There are certain laws that govern success, too. This means that success is not about being extra-smart, extra-talented, or extra-creative. And it's definitely not about starting a four-leafed clover collection or being endowed with a special success gene before you exit your mother's womb. Successful people aren't destined for success from birth, and they don't achieve success by accident. They don't become successful by copying what other people have already done, either. That strategy won't work, despite what some people like to say. You can learn a lot from people who have already achieved success, but you can never copy them completely. Every successful person has become successful in one way and one way only: by following the Laws of Success.

Every path to success will be different. Your path to success will be completely unique to you. It won't look exactly like anyone else's path. It will be different from mine, and both of our paths will be different from the next person's path. The only thing that all our different paths will have in common is that, to the extent that we each achieve success, we will do so by abiding by the same laws. This means that your path to success will depend on how well you understand the Laws of Success, and, more importantly, how well you're able to apply them to your life.

***

Earl Nightengale defined success as "the progressive realization of a worthy goal or ideal." This is an excellent definition. It captures well the commonly misunderstood character of success: success is not something you can possess; it is, ultimately, something you embody. Success is not simply about reaching a destination because, as you will find out, that destination will constantly move as you approach it. Rather, success is about making *consistent progress* toward your ideal life. It's completely up to you to decide what your ideal life looks like, and it's okay if your ideal life changes over time. Right now, your ideal life might include reaching a certain career level, achieving a target net worth, or having the freedom to travel the world. Someday it might include starting a family, earning a degree, buying a house, becoming an astronaut, or getting a dog. It doesn't matter what it is, as long as it's your ideal. Success for you will be your gradual realization of that ideal.

Keeping in mind that success is about making progress, it's also important to know that there is a Spectrum of Success. This spectrum has three main levels: below-average, average, and above-average. Your job, as someone who is pursuing success, is to make progress across this spectrum. You want to go from below-average to average, and then from average to above-average in every area of life. Most people will get stuck at some point along the spectrum and will end up spending most of their lives operating at a below-average or average level. Only a relatively small percentage of people will ever become above-average at anything. And an even smaller percentage of people will become above-average in every area of their lives. But the crucial thing to remember is that where you end up along the Spectrum of Success will be determined by one thing and one thing only: it will be determined by how well you align yourself with the Laws of Success.

People who are below-average at anything in life are so because they violate the Laws of Success. And, just as is the case with any law, when you violate the Laws of Success there are consequences. Violating the law of gravity by walking off a tenth-floor balcony, for example, will lead to some pretty serious physical pain, just as violating the law of supply and demand will lead to financial pain. The consequence of consistently violating the Laws of Success is simple: you will remain below-average. Most people who are below-average walk around every day with very little awareness that they are constantly sabotaging their own success by violating the very laws they should be following. If this is you, it's no wonder you feel frustrated: every time you take one step forward you take two steps back again. Violating the Laws of Success makes it impossible to succeed.

When it comes to people who are average, these people typically understand enough about the Laws of Success to keep themselves from getting too badly hurt by them most of the time. In other words, they understand enough to survive. That's why so many people are concerned mostly with "getting by." And so, they end up doing just enough to remain mediocre. They usually aren't consciously aware of the Laws of Success, but, either because of how they were brought up or through their own experience, they've managed to pick up some behaviors that prevent them from violating most of the laws most of the time.

However, there are two lies average people believe which prevent them from ever becoming above-average. The first is that they believe they're average. They claim to be "realistic" about who they are and what they can achieve. But, in reality, they have simply settled for what they currently have and lowered their expectations for their future. The second lie average people believe is that their only ticket to move up to the next level along the Spectrum of Success is hard work. They believe that they've achieved what they currently have through hard work and that the recipe for moving up to the next level is more of the same. These lies are dangerous because they completely block people who believe them from ever learning the truth— namely, that the way to move across the Spectrum of Success is not through quantity (doing more), but rather through quality (changing what you do and how you do it). In other words, these lies guarantee that those who believe them will remain average for their entire lives because they prevent those people from fully aligning themselves with the Laws of Success. If you feel like you are just "getting by" most of the time, that's a sure indication that you are currently operating at an average level.

People who are above-average at anything, however, are very different from everyone else. Above-average people focus on living their lives according to the Laws of Success every single day. They understand that the world always works according to very specific and predictable laws, and then they align themselves with those laws instead of against them. However, the most successful people don't just do their best to avoid violating the Laws of Success; they study those laws until they figure out how to harness their power and use them to propel them to where they want to go. By learning the specific laws that govern the road to success,

14

above-average people learn to use those laws to their advantage. That's how they set themselves apart from virtually everyone else. And that's how you will find success, too.

***

This book will introduce you to the forty-seven essential laws that determine where you end up along the Spectrum of Success. These laws will unlock success for you in virtually every area of life—if you understand them, follow them, and practice using them to your advantage. These laws are not about tapping into supernatural forces or conjuring results through magical spells. They are scientific in the sense that they simply describe the way success works. Whether they work for you will depend on how well you understand them and, most importantly, how hard you work to apply them in your life.

You will notice that there are a number of recurring themes woven through these laws. Some of the laws will include aspects that overlap with others. This is because the laws are all complimentary. They work together by building on each other and supporting one another. They form something like a kaleidoscope; only when understood in their totality will a clear picture of your path to success emerge.

Still, everyone will find some laws easier to apply or more relevant to their situation than other laws. We all have different needs and struggles. We are all at different stages of our journeys. This means that there are forty-seven different starting points you can take in this book, depending on your situation. So, when you get down to figuring out how these laws apply to all the unique nuances of your life, start with the ones that make the most sense for you right now, and don't yet worry about the ones that strike you as more difficult. Because all these laws work together, you will find that, as you begin to apply some of them to your life, it will become easier to apply others as well. My hope is that this book can serve as an ongoing resource that you can turn to as you face different challenges along your journey.

However, while every law you follow will pay dividends, in order to move into above-average territory in every area of your life you will want to work to follow as many of the laws as you can. If you manage to work your way up to following every single one of the laws I discuss in this book, you *will* have success. And, most likely, it will exceed your wildest dreams.

1. The Law of the Airplane

The airplane stays up because it doesn't have the time to fall.

—Orville Wright

T he Law of the Airplane states that success is achieved much more easily when you work in accordance *with* the Laws of Success, rather than against them. This first law is really a meta-law because it's a law that governs all the other laws in this book. As such, it is foundational for everything else that will come in the following pages. Yet, after working with people from every walk of life for well over a decade, I am amazed by how few people truly understand it. Almost every day I talk to people who tell me that they're eager to "shoot for the moon" in various areas of their lives and "skyrocket" their productivity. They have ambitious goals and they're determined to reach them. Some of these people go on to achieve great things; unfortunately, many others don't. In my experience, I have found that the single best predictor of success is whether or not a person abides by the Law of the Airplane. Those who do tend to find incredible success, while those who don't almost never make any serious progress toward their goals.

Before explaining the Law of the Airplane in detail, let me first illustrate why it is so important by telling you briefly about my friend, Jeremy. Jeremy was a good friend of mine. We worked together for a number of years, and we kept in touch well after our career paths parted. One day, when Jeremy and I were speaking on the phone, he told me that he had recently decided to make some serious changes in his life. He had been outside playing basketball with his teenage kids and, for the first time, he realized that he was in terrible shape. He was so out of shape that he couldn't physically finish the game. He felt embarrassed and a little scared about not being there for his kids later in life. So, in that moment, he decided to change his lifestyle. He was determined to lose weight by following a regimented exercise routine and a strict diet. He explained to me his exercise plan in detail, and he already knew what his meals would look like each week. I could tell that he was determined to make serious changes in his life.

About two months passed until I spoke with Jeremy again. As soon as I heard his voice on the phone, I knew something wasn't right. The last time I spoke with him, I could hear resolve in his voice. He was determined to make a change, and I could tell just by the sound of his voice. But this time his resolve was gone. Instead, he sounded defeated. I could tell right away that something was different. So, after some small chit-chat, I asked him how things were going with his diet and exercise plan. He told me that his new routine had lasted all of three weeks. He felt like a failure. He doubted whether it was even possible for him to get back in shape. He had resigned himself to the fact that being in shape was simply "not in the cards" for him.

As soon as I heard him talking like this, I knew exactly what was going on. So, I explained his problem in the simplest terms I could. I told him that he was trying to pursue his goal like a rocket ship, but that success most often requires an airplane. You see, it takes roughly ten times more fuel for a rocket to travel the same distance as an airplane. This means that you could fly nineteen times around the world in an airplane using the same amount of fuel you would need to fly to the moon and back in a rocket. If you've ever witnessed a rocket launch on TV, you'll know this is true. The amount of sheer force a rocket uses to launch and then cut through the atmosphere is incredible. An airplane uses some significant force to take-off as well, but nowhere near that needed by a rocket. And a plane uses even less once it reaches cruising altitude.

The main reason for this has to do with two factors: first, rocket engines don't use oxygen, which means they must generate their own substitute to make the engine run; and second, rockets don't use air to attain lift. In other words, rocket engines are designed to fight against gravity. They're designed to propel the rocket up, despite the force of gravity working to pull the rocket down.

Airplanes, on the other hand, not only use oxygen in their engines but they also use air to help them take-off and to keep them from crashing to the ground. Airplanes' wings essentially push air down, which in turn pushes the plane up. This creates what is called the force of lift. We know that when the force of lift is stronger than the force of gravity, the airplane will fly. It's a law. As long as the plane is travelling fast enough, it will continue to push air down and stay in flight. The quote at the beginning of this chapter from Orville Wright, one of the famous Wright brothers, is literally true: by working along with natural laws, the plane is not given enough time to fall. So, whereas a rocket essentially defies the law of gravity through propulsion, an airplane overcomes the pull of gravity by manipulating air pressure. The rocket defies natural laws; the airplane works along *with* them.

When it comes to achieving success, too often we try to rely only on some kind of inner propulsion. Maybe, like my friend Jeremy, something happens that makes you determined to reach a new goal. Maybe you see a picture of a friend that inspires you to get in shape. Or maybe you're desperate to prove someone wrong. These pieces of motivation can serve as your inner propulsion. And you should definitely use them because they will get you to take that first step and get you off the ground. After all, an airplane still needs propulsion; it just doesn't need as much as a rocket because it makes better use of air pressure. But these pieces of inner motivation almost certainly won't be enough to get you where you want to go. Being too out of shape was enough for Jeremy to sign up for a gym membership and plan a new diet. But it wasn't strong enough for him to beat his inner gravitational force, pulling him back to his comfortable life. Your desire to prove your mother wrong, for example, can be enough to get you through a difficult job interview, but it usually won't sustain your entire career.

You see, finding inner propulsion is a good thing. And successful people use as much of it as they can get. But, successful people also recognize that they need to work along with the Laws of Success in order to make it as far as possible. Just like an airplane uses propulsion *and* air pressure to fly, successful people know that they need to use inner motivation as propulsion *and* the Laws of Success in order to get where they want to go. Successful people know that it's much better to be an airplane than a rocket ship.

2. The Law of the Glass Ceiling

Whether you think you can or think you can't, you're right.

—Henry Ford

Τhe Law of the Glass Ceiling states that whatever you believe you can achieve is the ceiling that determines what you will accomplish. If you truly believe you can become a chess grandmaster, you might achieve that goal. But if you don't believe that it's possible for you, you certainly won't ever achieve it. You will never rise beyond what you believe you can be and achieve. In fact, the general rule is that you will most often achieve slightly less than you believe you can achieve. If your belief is at a six, for example, you will never rise beyond a five. If your belief is at a ten, you will likely hit a nine. Your level of belief in yourself, for better or worse, always determines your level of success.

Let me tell you a story to illustrate what I mean. About fifteen years ago, I met Crystal, who was a young, aspiring actress. Her dream was to make it big in Hollywood. And she wasn't afraid to tell people that she would be famous one day. But, for years, she had a day job in an office and lived in a small city in the Midwest. She managed to get a few roles here and there in commercials and local productions, but she never got her big break. For fifteen years, she spent most of her evenings hanging out with friends from work, and, on the weekends, she helped her mom with her small real estate business. Today, Crystal is a server at a restaurant in a city close to the town where she grew up. She married a nice guy she met at work, and they now have two small children. She hasn't had an acting job in a few years because she's been too busy. But she still claims to be waiting for her big break.

Judging from the outside, you might look at Crystal's story and think that she's lazy, or that she doesn't have the drive needed to succeed. Or you could conclude that she lacked the talent necessary to become a successful actress. I don't know if these things are true. We'll probably never know. But the thing I do know is that she's never been able to raise the glass ceiling she built for herself fifteen years ago. The main thing that prevented her from having greater success was her belief in herself. She never moved out to Hollywood because, deep down, she doubted whether she could actually make it. She settled for local acting jobs because, secretly, she thought these jobs were as good as it could get for her. She moved to the city just down the street from her small town because, for her, that meant she had achieved something. She passed up on auditioning for bigger roles because she didn't believe she had a chance of landing them. For Crystal, Hollywood was always a dream, but it wasn't the kind of dream that would come true for someone like her. She's never fully believed that she can make it in Hollywood, and so she never will.

Crystal's glass ceiling is built out of her limiting beliefs. These are the beliefs she has about herself and her world that hold her back. She believes that successful actresses in Hollywood don't come from small towns. She believes that people from her family don't become famous. She believes that moving to a new city is hard. She believes that she doesn't have the right look to succeed in Hollywood. And there are hundreds of other things she believes that hold her back. She would probably never say any of these things out loud. She might not even recognize that she's thinking them. But, deep down, they're there and they're holding her back.

We all have limiting beliefs that shape what we think is possible for us. You might not want to become a famous actress, but I guarantee that you have limiting beliefs keeping you from reaching your goals. Maybe you believe that you're too young for success, or you're too old to start again. Maybe you believe that there's no way for someone like you to escape the rat race. Maybe you believe that you're average at your job, or that you don't have the right background or experience. Whatever your limiting beliefs are, they're holding you back.

In his excellent book, *The Big Leap*, clinical psychologist, Gay Hendricks, explains that the limiting beliefs we have not only hold us back from reaching our full potential but actively sabotage our attempts to find success in life. This explains why, according to Hendricks, when something good happens to us in one area of our lives, we often do things that are destructive in other areas. For example, after winning the employee of the month award at work, you might come home and pick a fight with your husband. Or, after making a big sale, you get a speeding ticket. On the surface, these events don't seem related. After all, there's probably a perfectly reasonable explanation for the fight you have with your husband. And there's no way making a sale could lead to a speeding ticket, right?

Wrong.

According to Hendricks, your mind will do anything to keep you at the level it has been programmed for. This principle is sometimes referred to as the principle of your internal thermostat. The idea is that, just like how a thermostat regulates the temperature in your home, so also your brain regulates your level of success. If the temperature dips too low in the winter, your furnace will automatically start up and bring your house back to the right temperature. Similarly, if your home becomes too hot in the summer, the thermostat sends a signal for the air conditioner to kick in and bring the temperature back down to where it's supposed to be.

Just like programming a thermostat, what you believe about yourself and your world programs your brain for the level of success it will work to maintain in your life. This is an automatic process; it happens without you being conscious of it. When you achieve success that rises above what you've programmed yourself for, your brain will regulate this success by bringing you back to the level you've previously set. Whether it's picking a fight, getting a speeding ticket, sleeping through a meeting, or any other number of destructive behaviors, these are the ways your brain tries to maintain homeostasis.

While there are countless beliefs that contribute to your glass ceiling, just as there are countless beliefs contributing to mine, working along with the Law of the Glass Ceiling means that you need to constantly work on raising that ceiling by challenging your limiting beliefs. We all have a ceiling. We all have limits. The difference between successful people and unsuccessful people is that successful people work to raise that ceiling every day. If you can push it just a smidge higher each and every day, you will be surprised how fast your life turns around.

Now, I realize that raising your glass ceiling is much easier said than done. This is, at least in part, because your glass ceiling resides in your unconscious. The psychiatrist, David Hawkins, has explained it like this: "The unconscious will allow us to have only what we believe we deserve. If we have a small view of ourselves, then what we deserve is poverty. And our unconscious will see to it that we have that actuality." Hawkins is right. The vast majority of what we do and what we think is operated by our subconscious selves. Some think that as much as 95% of everything we do, say, and think comes from our subconscious.

But simply being aware of the glass ceiling and the fact that raising it is possible is the most important first step. When you do start raising that glass ceiling, that's when you can begin to see the effects of your glass ceiling in your life. You can begin to catch yourself when limiting thoughts pop into your head seemingly out of nowhere. You can interrogate those thoughts and figure out where they come from. What limiting beliefs are sitting in your unconscious that produced them? You can begin to think more critically about what you say and do as well. As you begin to think more critically about the things you think, say, and do, you will begin to see evidence of your glass ceiling popping up everywhere, like weeds in a garden. And, just like pulling weeds, you can use the bits above the surface to trace them down to their roots.

If you start doing this, you will not be able to help but make serious progress toward your goals. However, it's important to remember that, while raising your level of belief is *necessary* for success, it isn't *sufficient*. In other words, you will not find success without a raised glass ceiling, but simply raising the ceiling will not automatically bring you success. You need to pair your raised ceiling with the other Laws of Success.

3. The Law of the Hero and the Author

The moment you take responsibility for everything in your life is the moment you can change anything in your life.

—Hal Elrod

The Law of the Hero and the Author states that responsibility is necessary for success. In order to have success, you must first take full responsibility for where you are and for getting where you want to go. The well-known psychologist and motivational speaker, Denis Waitley, put it well: "There are two primary choices in life: To accept conditions as they exist, or accept the responsibility for changing them." You must choose one or the other. And the choice is completely up to you.

The reason this law is so important is because you cannot have control over your life without first taking responsibility for your circumstances. In fact, when it comes to achieving success, *responsibility is control*. This means that, if you don't ever take full responsibility for the circumstances you currently find yourself in, you will never be able to change them. If you're not the one responsible when you find yourself working at a job you hate, engaged in a string of failed relationships, or making less money than you want (and these things *will* happen), you're not the one with the power to change those situations.

It's not always easy to take responsibility for the parts of our lives that aren't quite the way we would like them to be. That's why a lot of people hate this law. They don't want their circumstances to be their fault. If that's you, don't feel too bad. It's not easy shouldering the blame for the things in your life that aren't going well. Nobody likes to be told that it's their fault that things haven't worked out the way they want. It's natural to want to blame our parents, our boss, our education, or our friends. I get that. I feel that too sometimes.

But, whether you like it or not, the reality is that every time you make someone else responsible, you relinquish control of your life. As soon as you blame the weather, the traffic, or your boss, you give them control. Now *they* have to change in order for your life to improve. And we all know that's probably not going to happen. If the reason you're not succeeding at your job is because of your boss, then the only way you can start to find success is if your boss changes. If the thing holding you back is the fact that your father doesn't believe in you, then the only way that you can start to achieve anything is if your father suddenly starts believing in you. Imagine banking your entire future on the hopes that someone else will change to make things easier on you! It might sound silly, but that's what a lot of us do. You see, the person who is in control—that is, the person who is responsible—is the one who determines the direction your life will take. It's up to you who you put in control of your life.

A helpful way to think about this is in terms of your life story. We are all naturally wired to think of our lives as stories. Your unique story began when you were born. Everything you've done, said, seen, thought, and felt from that moment is part of your story. Just like everyone else's story, your life story has ups and downs, and highs and lows. There are parts of your story where you've been sad, and other parts where you've been happy. There are parts where you've succeeded, and parts where you've failed. Just like any story, there are twists and turns.

Naturally, of course, because it's *your* story, you are the hero. The story of your life is about *you*. Every other character in your story—your spouse, children, colleagues, friends, parents—plays a supporting role. You are the only star of your story.

However, each life story is different. The story you are living is different from the one I'm living. And both of our stories are different from the ones Elvis Presley or Joan of Arc lived. Every story is unique. And here's a truth people often find difficult to hear: *some people are living better stories than other people*. We all know that some books are better than others. We recognize good books because they have a more dramatic climax than most books. They have more surprising twists and turns. They have more profound moments of suspense, heartache, and anger. They also have deeper moments of clarity, humor, and love. Every book is different, but really good books always have better stories than most other books.

But the most important thing that determines whether a book is considered a classic or trash is the plot. The plot is the central direction or purpose of the story. It's what guides and organizes all the little parts of the story together, and it's what gives the story meaning. A good plot will make you excited about where the story is going. It will make you want to read the book as fast as you can. A book with a good plot is the kind of book you stay up reading until 3 or 4 a.m. because you can't put it down. A book without a compelling plot, on the other hand, is just the opposite. Getting through even a single page can be an onerous task, as your brain reminds you constantly that you could be doing literally anything else. And so, while it can feel like it's impossible to put a book with a good plot down, it's almost impossible *not* to quit reading a book with a bad plot.

The story of your life is a lot like a book. It can be a good story, or it can be a bad story. Everyone's life story will include a lot of the same pieces—pain, betrayal, love, joy, and confusion. The main difference between a good life story and a life story that is mediocre is the plot. So, stop and think for a moment: What is the central plot of your life story? Is it a rags to riches story, where you start from the bottom but, against all odds, fight your way to the top? Is it a love story, where you sacrifice everything you have for the people you care most about? Is it a story of perseverance and survival, the triumph of the human spirit, where you continually face incredible opposition but you never give up to the end? There are a million different plotlines your story could follow. The question is: which one are you currently living?

Unfortunately, for most of us, the plot to our life story isn't very compelling. If we're honest, most of us probably find our own life story pretty boring. A lot of our life stories could be summed up something like this: we get up in the morning after a night of too little sleep, and we head off to jobs that don't fulfill us; we then come home to a list of chores, most of which we don't do, and flop ourselves on the couch, ready to fall asleep watching a show that's more interesting than the lives we're actually living; six hours later, we wake up and do the whole thing over again. I don't think most of us would continue to read a book that simply repeated this same boring day over and over again without some larger, more compelling plot. But, for most of us, there really is no larger plot. No wonder so many of us are less than enthused about the lives we lead.

Now, think with me for a minute. Who is able to turn a story from a boring dud to a page-turner? Is it the hero? No, it isn't. The only one who can take a story that sucks and craft it into something exciting and meaningful is the author. The hero might be the star of the story, but the author is the one in control. The author is the one who decides what will happen to the hero. The author decides how the hero will act and react. The author is the one who decides what the hero will want, and what steps the hero will take to get it. It's the author who is in control, not the hero.

The Law of the Hero and the Author recognizes that someone is always in control. There will always be an author of your life story. Every detail of your story that you don't design will be designed by someone else. If you're only the hero of your story, you will eventually figure out that you're actually spending your life as a supporting character in someone else's story.

The only solution is to decide to become the author. Being an author is not as glamorous as being the hero. It requires hard work that often goes unrecognized. But it also puts you in control of your story. Once you decide to become the author of your life story, you have the opportunity to get down to writing the best story you possibly can. You have the opportunity to turn your life into a page-turner.

Wouldn't it be nice to live a life like that? Wouldn't it be nice to be excited about getting up in the morning because you're wrapped up in wherever your story is heading? Most people live their lives like a boring novel—they're not excited about anything. Mayber they're apprehensive. They're dreading what comes next. It's like they're being forced to read a book they desperately want to put down. If that's you, remember: you can be the author. You can change your story. If your life is like a book you want to quit reading, you have the power to turn your life into a story fueled by excitement and anticipation.

There simply is no getting around this law. The more responsibility you take for your life, the greater your opportunities for success will be.

4. The Law of Exaptation

The notion of being 'for' something shouldn't be taken too seriously, if only because of the ubiquitous phenomenon of exaptation.

—Noam Chomsky

The Law of Exaptation states that success requires the application of skills and abilities in domains other than where they were initially developed. In other words, in order to have success, you need to be able to effectively and efficiently take the skills, abilities, and traits you learn in one area of life and apply them to a different area. The better you are able to do this, the greater degree of success you will achieve.

Exaptation is a term that originated in the field of evolutionary biology. It is used to refer to the process by which features that evolved for one purpose are then used for a different purpose. For example, biologists tell us that the human tongue evolved to help us capture and eat food. It was a survival mechanism to help prevent us from starving to death. But, over time the tongue came to be used for a very different purpose: communication. We developed the ability to speak to one another, which allowed us to begin to develop highly complex social relationships. This, in turn, enabled us to develop standards for communication by crafting complex language patterns. Eventually, based on the language we were speaking, we developed ways of writing our language down. And this ability to communicate through writing required that we develop entirely new cognitive processes. This led to our ability to think abstractly. So, even though the tongue was not initially meant for this purpose, being able to apply it to something else—namely, communication—has turned out to be one of the most important developments in our evolutionary history. I would not have been able to write this book, and you would not be able to read it, without exaptation.

However, the principle of exaptation does not only refer to biologically determined developments. It has also been used to refer to psychological and social developments as well. We use exaptation in a wide range of everyday behaviors. And these behaviors can often be harnessed and used to achieve success in a variety of different domains in our lives. I have seen my friend, Katie, who has a graduate degree in art history become very successful in the business world. She doesn't use her knowledge of art history every day, but she leans on her ability to do in-depth research quickly and efficiently in order to give her an advantage in the company she works for. I have known retired military personnel who rely on the discipline they developed during their time in the military to get up at 4 a.m. every day and work on their business before the demands of the day start rolling in. They are not necessarily the best business minds, but they have figured out a way to harness the skills they do possess to make up for other skills they might lack.

Using the Law of Exaptation to your advantage means learning how to achieve success by leveraging *your* unique knowledge, skillset, and abilities. Successful people don't learn the ins and outs of everything they pursue. Rather, they maximize their ability to use the Law of Exaptation so that they can achieve success by relying on the things they're already good at, regardless of the context.

There are two main steps needed to harness the power of exaptation. The first thing you need to do is you need to get reasonably good at something. You don't need to be the best in the world at that thing. But you need to be above average. The good thing is that most of us are already at least close to above average at something, whether we know it or not. So, you probably just need to figure out what that thing is and improve on it further, if needed.

The reason why it's important to begin by getting good at something is because being good at anything requires you to develop a whole bunch of smaller skills. For example, to become good at playing the piano, you don't actually develop some skill called "playing the piano." You develop a whole set of smaller skills that you then use to play the piano. You develop the ability to read music, keep rhythm, recognize pitch, and play scales and chords. You will also need to understand something about the mechanics of the piano and music theory. There are probably at least a hundred other related things you need to learn to do in order to be able to play the piano well. And you could break down each of those smaller skills into even smaller skills. Learning music theory, for example, means that you have to be able to think mathematically, and playing scales means that you have to develop a certain amount of finger dexterity. When you think about it like this, setting out to learn the piano actually means that you are setting out to learn a large set of small skills that you will use to play the piano.

This means that what you think you're good at right now is probably not really what you're good at. You might think that you're good at being a server, for example, because you earn more tips than your co-workers. But, in reality, you're actually receiving those tips because you have figured out how to apply a bunch of smaller skills to your job. Maybe you've developed strong interpersonal skills, which cause patrons to like you. Or maybe you've developed a sharp working memory, which allows you to keep a lot of complex orders straight in your head. Once again, there's no such thing as having the skill of serving drinks or food, even though we commonly talk like there is. In reality, being a good server simply means that you've figured out how to use a bunch of smaller skills effectively in the context of a restaurant.

When you think about every skill you possess like this, a whole new world opens up. When you understand that everything you learn to "do" is really a matter of using a bunch of smaller skills to achieve a particular outcome, you will begin to see all kinds of possibilities. You can become really good at playing the piano or serving drinks simply by identifying the particular skills you are using for those tasks and focusing on improving them incrementally. This is essentially what focused practice is.

But, more importantly, all of the small skills you learn "for" playing the piano or waiting tables could also be used to help you in other areas of life. Once you begin to see that what you initially thought your skills were "for" is just one of countless ways you can apply them, you will begin to see the possibilities the Law of Exaptation opens up for you.

This brings us to the second step you need to take to harness the power of exaptation. This step involves the ability to recognize opportunities for exaptation. In order to be able to use the Law of Exaptation to your advantage, it's not enough to know that every skill you possess is made up of a bunch of smaller skills that can be transferred to other domains. You must also be able to recognize opportunities to apply those skills for your benefit. To do this, you will need to practice breaking down big skills into their smaller pieces. Not only do you need to do this to fully understand the range of skills you possess, but you also need to be able to do this to figure out where you might be able to apply those skills for your benefit. My friend, Katie, would never have been able to apply her research skills to the business world if she wasn't able to recognize that she possessed skills she could apply in that world in the first place. She was able to recognize this because she thought carefully about all the small skills needed to succeed in business, and she compared them with all the small skills she developed in graduate school. She knew that, just like there's no such thing as being good at graduate school, there's no such thing as being good at business. She recognized that, in order to succeed at business, you need a bunch of smaller skills. And, because she was able to identify these smaller skills, she was then able to figure out which of these skills she could bring to the table.

There's a double-benefit that comes from getting good at recognizing opportunities for exaptation. Not only does it help you recognize how you can apply the skills you currently have to new things, but it also helps you identify additional skills you might want to develop. Katie knew that she could bring the ability to do high-quality research to the business world, but this didn't mean that she didn't have to develop any new skills. She still needed to learn the language and concepts that would enable her to navigate the business world, for example. So, she spent some time researching the business world and talking with business people. Eventually, she felt comfortable in that world, and when she had the opportunity to pitch herself, she was able to speak their language. The Law of Exaptation does not completely eliminate the need to gain additional knowledge and develop additional skills. But it does provide opportunities to significantly shorten the learning curve needed to succeed.

As the quote from Noam Chomsky suggests at the beginning of this chapter, we would do well to refrain from thinking too narrowly about what the various skills we develop are "for." When we think that all the smaller skills we learn as we learn to play piano are *for* playing the piano, we run the risk of violating the Law of Exaptation. And when we violate the Law of Exaptation, we miss out on a wide range of opportunities to use the skills we've developed in all kinds of interesting ways.

In the end, the more skills you have, the better it will be for exaptation. This is why accruing a large skillset is always a good idea, regardless of what you might have initially thought each of these skills were "for." You might not know what you will use each individual skill for in the end, but the point is that you can always use every skill for multiple things. In fact, if you're doing it right, it's almost a guarantee that what you end up using your skills for will be very different from the reasons you initially acquired them. If you want to find success, you need to follow the Law of Exaptation.

5. The Law of Initial Value

When you are prepared for a thing, the opportunity to use it presents itself.

—Edgar Cayce

The Law of Initial Value states that success is determined by what happens when internal preparation meets external opportunity. It dictates that internal preparation always precedes your ability to achieve success. In other words, you must be internally prepared *before* opportunities arise in order to be able to take advantage of them. This means that, *ultimately, the level of success you achieve will be determined by the value you bring to the opportunities that arise.*

The Law of Initial Value is based on a book published by the Austrian scientist and psychiatrist, Joseph Wilder, entitled, *Stimulus and Response: The Law of Initial Value.* In this book, Wilder recounts the findings of a series of experiments he conducted throughout the 1920s. In these experiments, he injected human subjects with either pilocarpine, atropine, or adrenaline, all of which are known to affect a subject's heart rate and blood pressure. At the time when he was conducting these experiments, it was widely assumed by scientists and physicians alike that any drug or medicine would have the same effect on every subject, provided the dosage remained consistent. In other words, it was assumed that, if you and I were both given the same dosage of adrenaline or atropine, our heartrates would both increase at the same rate. And, likewise, if we were given the same amount of pilocarpine, it would have been expected that our heartrates would decrease at the same rate.

But Wilder's experiments yielded some surprising results. He found that the effect of each substance varied quite dramatically among his subjects. By monitoring each subject's pulse and blood pressure, Wilder found that the effect of each injection was, more or less, inversely proportionate to the value the subject had in their bodies prior to the injection. In other words, he found that people who naturally had a higher level of adrenaline in their bodies before the experiment began were less affected by the shot of adrenaline he gave them. On the other hand, he found that, for those who had a lower level of adrenaline in their bodies to begin with, the dosage of adrenaline he gave them increased their heartrate and blood pressure much more dramatically. He observed the same pattern at work in those who received injections of pilocarpine and atropine as well.

After conducting a number of other experiments to confirm his findings, Wilder concluded that he had discovered a natural, biological law, which he suspected was present in every living organism. Thus, he formulated what has become known as Wilder's Law of Initial Value. He defined the law like this: "The direction of response of a body function to any agent depends to a large degree on the initial level of that function." Put more plainly, while each medicine will, more or less, have the same kind of effect on every person, it will not effect every person to the same degree. The degree to which the medicine is effective will be determined by the condition, or "initial value," of the person's body before they receive it. Thus, those who have a high level of initial value of adrenaline will not be as dramatically affected by an adrenaline injection as those who have a low level of initial value at the time of injection. This law, Wilder concluded, is at work any time a living organism is introduced to any stimulating substance.

This law works because a healthy living organism will always react in one of two ways when it is introduced to a new substance: it will either try to absorb the substance into the organism, or it will reject the substance and attempt to expel it from the body. Every time you ingest healthy food that your body can use to survive and grow, your body naturally absorbs that food. This is how you literally become what you eat. However, whenever you ingest something your body cannot use, it works like mad to expel that thing. We've all had the unpleasant experience of eating something, only to bring it back up some time later. That's an example of how the body rejects certain substances it determines to be harmful or unhelpful.

Now, a really fascinating thing about our bodies is that they can learn to absorb substances they might have previously rejected and vice versa. Suppose you eat an unhealthy diet filled with junk food. Your body will be used to this diet, and so it will absorb the food you give it, which will have some unhealthy consequences. But, now suppose that you drastically change your diet, and you eat nothing but fresh fruits, vegetables, lentils, and fish for an entire year. After that year, your body will not be as good at absorbing junk as it used to be. You will find that, if you do try to return to your previous diet of junk food, you will feel your body trying to reject it. This is because your body learns what to accept and what to reject based on what you teach it.

While Wilder was concerned with the application of this law exclusively within the scientific realm, we can find this same law at work on social and psychological levels as well. Receiving an excellent grade, for example, will often have a more dramatic effect on a student who is used to getting Cs, while it will have a less dramatic effect on a student who is used to getting straight As. In this case, the two students are given the same positive information, but its impact is much stronger on one than the other because each student brought a different level of initial value to the experience. The student who is used to getting Cs brings a lower level of initial value, psychologically and emotionally speaking, than the student used to getting As in every class. Therefore, the effect of receiving an A in one class will be dramatically more substantial for the C student than it will be for the A student.

Similarly, coming into a windfall of cash, whether by receiving an inheritance or winning the lottery, will predictably have a more dramatic impact on a person if they were not well-off to begin with. A person who was previously wealthy, on the other hand, will typically not be affected as dramatically. The reason is not because the money is somehow less valuable to the wealthy person. It's not even because it's more useful to the person who isn't wealthy. Rather, the difference is that the wealthy person has a higher level of initial value, and so the effect of more money does not impact them to the same degree.

In both cases, having a higher level of initial value provides an advantage. The straight A student is much more likely to continue to be a straight A student and the wealthy person will almost certainly use their new money to increase their wealth. But we know, statistically speaking, it is almost a guarantee that the C student will revert right back to getting Cs in their next class and that the unwealthy person will eventually spend their money and return to their previous standard of living.

It can be very tempting to look at situations like these and assume that the A student receives As because they're smarter, or that the wealthy person uses their new money to increase their wealth because they're not as desperate for the cash. But that would be wrong. The real difference between the A student and the C student, or between the wealthy person and the unwealthy person, is psychological. In other words, the A student is not an A student because she receives As in every class; she receives As in every class because *she's* an A student. She acts, thinks, works, believes in a way that results in her being at the top of her class. Similarly, the wealthy person isn't wealthy because he has a lot of money; he has a lot of money because he's a wealthy *person*. This law is, in many ways, the flipside of the Law of the Glass Ceiling, which I have already discussed. The important point here is that the external result is only a symptom of internal preparation. And that internal preparation must precede the opportunity in order to be able to take advantage of it.

Because both the A student and the wealthy person have prepared themselves properly, they are able to take advantage of opportunities when they arise. The C student was given an amazing opportunity. They could have reverse engineered the process to figure out exactly what they did differently that earned them the higher mark and then applied that same process moving forward to raise their grades in all their future courses. If you get Cs in every class, it can be very difficult to figure out exactly what needs to be done to improve your grades. But, receiving an A is the perfect opportunity to figure that out. Similarly, making a lot of money usually requires a smaller sum of money first, and so the unwealthy person was given an incredible opportunity to make more money, if they only took the time to invest it properly. But, people who find themselves in these situations almost never take advantage of these opportunities. Instead, they revert back to their previous ways and continue to think success is about luck or privilege.

Any time you treat success like a fluke, like something you don't deserve, you reveal that you have a low level of initial value. Any time you see small successes as ends instead of opportunities to achieve bigger successes, you violate the Law of Initial Value. As a result, the successes you do experience (and we all experience successes) become ends in themselves, rather than opportunities for more success. Because the unwealthy person is not prepared for money, when the get some they treat it like it's an end in itself. A wealthy person, on the other hand, recognizes that extra money opens up more opportunities to make even more. And so they compound little successes into big successes.

When you act like a C student or an unwealthy person, you violate the Law of Initial Value. People who aren't prepared to handle opportunities when they come their way tend to think of success as something beyond their reach. And, if, by some miracle, they ever achieve a little of it, it ends up being a single blip on the screen of their lives.

Working along with the Law of Initial Value means working to ensure that you are in the best psychological and emotional state to recognize opportunities and make the most of them when they come along. This is why truly successful people know that you should always work harder on yourself than you do on your job. Successful people know that, if you make sure that *you* are constantly growing and increasing your initial value, you will achieve success.

The practical lesson is that you should always be on the lookout for opportunities to improve your skillset and mindset. The first and most important way to begin to raise your initial value is to be mindful of what you are inputting to yourself. Who are you spending your time with? Are they C students? Are they bad with money? Are they unsuccessful in the areas that matter most to you? What are you spending your time watching, reading, and listening to? Does it help you increase your initial value by challenging you, or does it keep you stuck in old patterns of thinking? What skills are you actively developing in your life? Are they the kinds of skills that will help you compound your successes in some way?

If you are constantly watching cat videos online, you shouldn't expect to increase your initial value very much. But, if you spend that time reading books about the stock market or personal development, not only will you become a smarter investor and more self-aware, you will probably be able to think just a bit more critically about many other things in your life as well. You will have increased the initial value you bring to any opportunity because you're increasing your ability to think strategically and reflectively. If you listen to music when you're commuting to work, you might enjoy your ride. But you won't increase your skills in any significant way. However, if you use that time to listen to a podcast on productivity, for example, you will expand your initial value by picking up tips and tricks that will help you get more of the most important things done. These are just some obvious examples, but there are plenty of others. The point is that, if you want to be able to harness the power of the Law of Initial Value, you will need to work on proactively increasing your initial value. Once you do this, you will find that small opportunities start leading to big opportunities. And that's where you will start to see success.

6. The Law of Transformation

Success is best measured by personal transformation, not growth in numbers.

—Robb Holman

The Law of Transformation states that any change in external circumstances requires an equal and proportionate change in internal constitution. In other words, you cannot achieve success—however you define it—without transforming who you are. This doesn't mean that you have to change your interests or your personality completely. It simply means that, if you want to achieve something you've never achieved before, something about you needs to change. Your current mindset and skillset have produced your current results. So, if you want different results, you need to change something about your mindset or skillset. And, the bigger the change you want to see in your life, the greater the inner transformation you must undergo.

This law is closely related to the Law of Initial Value from the previous chapter. However, while that law was focused on the importance of preparing yourself for opportunities to have success, this law goes deeper by focusing on how success requires a transformation of who you are.

The great entrepreneur and motivational speaker, Jim Rohn, used to say that everyone should have the goal of becoming a millionaire. He didn't say this because having money is all that important. In fact, he used to tell people that they could give it all away after they earn it, if that's what they wanted to do. The reason why he recommended that everyone have a goal of becoming a millionaire was because, for most people, achieving millionaire status requires a substantial personal transformation. You need to become a different person in order to be a millionaire. You simply cannot go about your life in exactly the same way as you have for the past twenty years and just expect a million dollars to fall into your lap. No, you need to make some pretty drastic changes to the way you think, make decisions, spend your time, set your priorities, and develop your skillset. Making a million dollars is a good goal because of what it requires you to become in order to achieve it.

There are two sides to this advice, and both are valuable. First, this advice makes it clear that the real value of success is not found in the rewards you receive but in the person you become. The personal transformation that success demands is always more valuable than any external reward you might receive. External things might make some parts of your life easier, but they will never fulfill you. Every successful person has learned this lesson at some point in their lives.

But the second side to this advice is also very important: there can be no success without personal transformation. Your transformation is not just a happy by-product of success; it is a prerequisite. This means that, if you want to take your success seriously, you need to pay particularly close attention to your own personal transformation. You need to work on controlling and optimizing how you think, how you act, and how you feel. Successful people tend to see the world differently in many ways. They react to setbacks and successes differently than average people, and they control their emotions in ways most people have never mastered.

This is, by far, one of the least understood Laws of Success. Success doesn't happen externally; it happens internally. If you want to be in a different place in your life ten years, two years, or two months from now, you need to focus first and foremost on your own personal transformation. Think about it like this. We all face challenges in our lives. The reason you are not where you want to be is because you haven't been able to overcome certain challenges. These challenges could be relational, financial, intellectual, or emotional. It doesn't matter. It's always the case that the reason you aren't where you want to be is because you have not yet been able to overcome at least one particular challenge in your life.

It's like knowing where you want to go, but there's a mountain that stands between you and your destination. The only way to get where you want to go is to overcome the challenge before you: you need to climb the mountain. But, what if you're not a mountain climber? Well, you'll need to become one. There's no other way. The first few steps up the mountain might not be that tough. But, eventually, you'll come to some difficult part that requires skills you don't yet have. You'll need to learn those skills, and possibly improve some old skills. You'll have to develop some different patterns of thinking and possibly an entirely new mindset. When you're scaling a mountain, you cannot act as if you are standing on flat ground. To get to the top, you need to become a different person. You need to become the kind of person who *can* climb the mountain.

This is always the case in life; there is always a mountain between where you are and where you want to go. Your job is always to improve yourself to the point where you're able to scale that mountain as quickly and efficiently as possible. You might need new relational, financial, intellectual, or emotional skills. But, as you begin to develop these skills in your life, you will be able to overcome whatever challenge is currently standing between you and your goal.

Your journey to success will always be a journey of personal transformation. Success is not just a matter of doing more of the same. It's not just a matter of productivity. Success is always about changing who you are so you can do what you've never done before. If the path before you looks impossible, it very well might be—based on who you are today. But, if you grow just a little today, you might become the kind of person who is able to take a step or two up your mountain tomorrow. And, if you grow a little more tomorrow, you might become the kind of person who can take a few more steps. And so on. One day, you will look back and realize that you've become a different person—you will have become a person who can scale the mountain standing between you and your dreams. And then, from the summit, you will look down and have your end goal clearly in sight.

7. The Law of Use

We must use what we have to invent what we desire.
—Adrienne Rich

T he Law of Use states that ability will expand when used but diminish if unused. There is no such thing as standing still in life. You are either moving toward your goals or away from them. You are either creating success or failure. You are either growing or shrinking. Every time you use whatever skills you have, you strengthen them. Every time you take advantage of an opportunity, you increase the number of additional opportunities that will come your way. But, as soon as you stop using your skills, you begin to lose them. There is a success feedback loop. And understanding the Law of Use is essential for ensuring you are able to use this feedback loop to your advantage.

People who work out regularly or play competitive sports will already know how the Law of Use impacts physical performance. Even if you're in better shape than anyone else in the world, it only takes a few days of inactivity for your ability to begin to diminish. The first thing to go is your cardio. And, after a couple of weeks, you will notice that you have lost significant muscle strength as well.

If you were to lay in your bed for six months without ever getting up, your muscles would atrophy to the point where your body may not ever be able to stand upright again. When it comes to the human body, we all know that you must use it or lose it.

But this law is applicable to everything in our lives, including love, gratitude, confidence, and motivation. Let me tell you a story about two best friends, Jen and Stacy. One New Year's Eve, Jen and Stacy came up with the bright idea of making a New Year's resolution together: they decided to run a marathon during the upcoming year. They talked a lot about how they've each wanted to do it for years, but just never got around to getting serious about it. They decided that this was the year to finally get serious about it. Neither one of them knew anything about running—and definitely nothing about running a marathon. But they were excited, and both of them went home motivated to get to work.

When Jen got home that night, she was tired, but she was too excited to sleep. She had to do something to calm herself down, so she started watching a movie until she drifted off to sleep. When she got up the next day, the first thing she thought about was how excited she was to start training for her marathon. She thought about all the days ahead where she would wake up before the crack of dawn to head out for a run. She was looking forward to it. But, on this particular day, Jen had a few errands to run. The whole time she was out, she kept thinking about what it would actually feel like to run a marathon. This was something she had been wanting to do for so long, it was almost surreal to think that, in just a few short months, she would actually be a marathon runner.

The next week was a pretty busy week for Jen at work. She had some important deadlines, and her boss had just made her the lead on her first major project. She needed to focus all her attention on her work for the next few weeks, if she wanted to prove that she could take on even bigger projects in the future. It was a big couple weeks for her career. During these weeks, Jen thought often about the marathon, but she forced herself to push it to the back of her mind each time so she could focus her full attention on work.

After about three weeks, she could finally lift up her head and take a breath. It had been the most difficult three weeks of her life. She had been working around the clock to make sure everything was perfect. And, now that the bulk of the work was over, she felt good.

She began to allow herself to think about the marathon again. She thought about how much work she had just put in for the past three weeks, and she began to wonder whether she would really want to put in all the work needed to run a whole marathon. She didn't know how much training she was supposed to do, but she figured that it's probably a lot.

She decided to give Stacy a call. Things were so busy for Jen at work over the past few weeks that the two friends hadn't been able to touch base beyond a few text messages since their big New Year's resolution. She wanted to see if Stacy's motivation was beginning to wane as well.

To Jen's surprise, she found that Stacy was even more motivated to run the marathon than she had been three weeks earlier. Stacy explained that, when she got back to her place on New Year's Eve, she, too, was too excited to sleep. But, instead of turning on a movie, Stacy spent a few hours that night researching how to train for a marathon. She found out that most people take around twenty weeks of pretty intense training to be ready, so she set out a plan and timeline she would need to follow in order to be ready for the marathon that was being held in September. She even located a handful of potential trainers in her city that she could call to help her along.

Stacy acted on her motivation immediately. And, as a result, it continued to grow. While Jen was putting her marathon aspirations on hold for three weeks, Stacy was going out for short runs every day. She wasn't running marathons yet, but she was getting used to becoming a runner. And it made her feel good. Every day she went out for a run, it was like she was filling up her motivation tank just a little bit more. After three weeks, Jen had done nothing and was ready to give up. Stacy, meanwhile, was already well on her way to accomplishing her goal.

In the end, Jen never even started training for the marathon. Stacy, on the other hand, completed her training as she had planned and finished the marathon that year. She enjoyed the process so much that she has continued to run one marathon every year since.

The deciding difference between the two was that Stacy *used* the little motivation she had right away, while Jen tried to store her motivation for a later date. But you cannot store motivation. If you don't use it, it will disappear. If you do use it, however, it will grow. The simple fact that Stacy used her motivation from day one meant that she was able to continually increase her motivation for the next eight months. Because Stacy chose not to use her motivation, it eventually evaporated completely. This illustrates well the Law of Use.

This law is applicable in practically every area of life. There are some skills you can learn that are very difficult to forget, such as painting or holding a conversation. We often like to say that using these skills is "like riding a bike." This is because, once you've learned how to balance, while also peddling and steering a bike, it's a skill you never really lose.

But have you ever gone a couple years without riding a bike? Sure, you remember how to do it, but it still feels pretty weird the first time you try to ride again. You might be a little wobbly, and it might take a little while before you feel comfortable again. Similarly, if you stop being creative, you will eventually find that you are not able to do the same creative activities you used to do. Or, if you go a long time alone without speaking to anyone, you will feel awkward around others for a while until you get yourself back in social shape. Even when it comes to the skills that you can supposedly never lose, your ability will decrease if you don't use them.

The same holds true with skills that might not always seem so obvious but are important for your success. There's the skill of taking advantage of opportunities, for example. People who are successful have to be good at taking advantage of opportunities. But if you pass up opportunities for a while, it won't take long for you to lose your edge. You might end up having to make a few bad decisions before you get yourself back into shape. You might find that you stop attracting good opportunities altogether. The same is true when it comes to the skill of generating ideas. Every successful person has to have some reasonably good ideas at some point. But unless you exercise your idea muscle, as it were, you will actually lose your ability to come up with good ideas.

The good news is that the opposite is also true. If your skills diminish when unused, exercising these skills makes you better at them. Just like how working out specific muscle groups will make you stronger, so also using skills will make you better at them. According to the Law of Use, therefore, success will come to those who use what they have more often than those who don't.

In order to harness the Law of Use to your advantage, the key is simple: look for every possible opportunity to use your skills and abilities, and don't ever fall into the trap of trying to store them up for later.

8. The Law of Resistance

Difficulties strengthen the mind, as labor does the body.

—Seneca

The Law of Resistance states that the level of success you achieve will be directly proportionate to the level and force of resistance you work to overcome. There is no such thing as achieving success without facing resistance. In fact, if you never experience resistance, you will never experience success. And, the more resistance you face, the greater your success will be when you do achieve it.

Resistance can come in many forms. It can come in the form of a little voice inside your head telling you you're not good enough. It can come in the form of physical discomfort making you want to give up. It can come in the form of various personal circumstances that make you think you'll never make it. Or it can come in about a thousand other forms. In his highly popular book, *The War of Art*, Steven Pressfield describes resistance as a universal force hell-bent on keeping everything exactly the way it is. Any time you attempt to do something that will improve some aspect of your life, you can bet that resistance will be there to greet you.

In some ways, you can think of resistance as the price you pay for success. It's like working out. If you want to build muscle, you need to use weights to provide resistance to your muscles. Your body won't build muscle naturally unless you use resistance. The burn you feel when you work out is not exactly pleasant, but it's a sure sign that it's working.

Much like how the price you pay for an item is usually related to the value of the item, so also the amount of resistance you experience is tied to the level of success you aim at. Getting out of bed in the morning after a late night can be difficult. You might feel like you have to use every last ounce of energy you have to overcome that resistance trying to keep you in bed. But, while it's nice to get out of bed, most of us probably would consider this a very minor success. You wouldn't be bragging about it with your friends later. But, as you pursue higher aims, the amount of resistance you face will increase as well. For example, starting a business is difficult. The amount of resistance involved at every step along the way is a million times more than the resistance you feel when you're lying in bed trying to muster the strength to roll out in the morning. But the success you achieve by overcoming the resistance is a million times better, too. As the value of the outcome increases, the price increases as well.

But resistance isn't just a necessary evil. It's also a necessary good. In his recent book, *The Comfort Crisis*, Michael Easter shows how the comforts we enjoy today are leading to urgent physical and mental health issues. Our temperature-controlled cars and homes, overflowing cupboards, instant access to unlimited entertainment, and streamlined paths to a livable wage all work to reduce the effects of resistance in our lives. While our ancestors were constantly faced with resistance on all fronts—weather, predators, poverty, the threat of starvation—we, by comparison, have it easy. He makes the case that the life of comparative comfort most of us lead has meant that we are lacking something essential for our physical and mental well-being: resistance.

Easter's book is a very helpful reminder that we all *need* resistance. We're wired for it. We need to be challenged. If you have days when you feel directionless or unmotivated, the solution could be as simple as finding a way to insert more resistance into your life. It might seem counterintuitive at first. But, once you understand the Law of Resistance, you can see how it makes sense. If you think it's best to try and pursue success by experiencing as little resistance as possible, you're in for a rude awakening.

Psychologist Mihaly Csikszentmihalyi famously investigated "optimal experience" in his book, *Flow: The Psychology of Optimal Experience*. In this book, Csikszentmihalyi sets out to determine what kinds of experiences are the most satisfying and fulfilling for us. You might expect that we are most satisfied when all our needs are being met and we have time to relax. Or you might think we are most satisfied when we've achieved something great, such as getting a new job or buying a new car. But that's not what Csikszentmihalyi found. Instead, he found that the moments when we are most satisfied with our lives are the moments when we're fighting to overcome resistance:

> Contrary to what we usually believe, moments like-these, the best moments in our lives, are not the passive, receptive, relaxing times—although such

experiences can also be enjoyable, if we have worked hard to attain them. The best moments usually occur when a person's body or mind is stretched to its limits in a voluntary effort to accomplish something difficult and worthwhile. Optimal experience is thus something that we make happen. For a child, it could be placing with trembling fingers the last block on a tower she has built, higher than any she has built so far; for a swimmer, it could be trying to beat his own record; for a violinist, mastering an intricate musical passage. For each person there are thousands of opportunities, challenges to expand ourselves.

And so we face a bit of a catch 22: we need resistance; yet, resistance often blocks us from achieving success. At least that's how it appears. But the truth is actually a bit more complex. You see, most people wind up overemphasizing one side of this equation over the other. They either pile up difficult goals and attempt to achieve them by sheer determination, or they see resistance as the enemy and flee at the first whiff of it. But, as we learned in the Law of the Airplane, taking on too much resistance is not a wise strategy. And, as we've learned in the Law of Transformation, fleeing from resistance will mean that you end up never overcoming the challenges standing between you and your dreams. What is needed is the appropriate balance between the two: *you need to embrace as much resistance as you are able, but not more than you can manage.* This balance will be different for every person, and it will change as you progress through life. But it's important to get it right because getting this balance wrong necessarily means that you will wind up violating the Law of Resistance. And when you do that, success becomes nearly impossible.

Practically speaking, you can only find your perfect balance between too much resistance and not enough through trial and error. It will take some time and a lot of tweaking, but it can be done. Try tackling something a little bigger than you're comfortable with. Try taking on something that's just a little beyond your current abilities. Whatever this means to you in your life, just try it. See what happens. If you find that you're buckling under the resistance you face (you will be able to withstand much more than you probably think), then you need to back off just a little. If, on the other hand, you find that you're lacking motivation to even get started, or you find that you're "waiting for inspiration," it's very likely that you haven't taken on enough resistance. Toy around with it until you get a general sense of the range of resistance that's optimal for you.

Once you have a sense of the range of resistance that is best for you right now, you will begin abiding by the Law of Resistance instead of violating it. You can even begin to set goals for yourself based on the level of resistance you expect each goal to produce, and you can begin to evaluate your actions each day based on whether or not they produce the correct amount of resistance.

You are also then in a position where you can take things further and begin to harness the power of this law for your advantage. Much like lifting weights, when you push yourself just a little beyond your ideal range of resistance, your ability to withstand resistance will grow.

To do this, you cannot wait until you *feel* like doing the thing you want to do. The whole point of resistance is that it makes you not feel like doing it. The key is to act anyway.

As the Harvard psychologist, Jerome Bruner, has said, "You're more likely to act yourself into feeling, than feeling yourself into action." You won't *feel* like pushing yourself beyond the range of resistance that you're comfortable with—at least not at first. But, if you start doing it, you will find that your feelings of inspiration begin to follow.

And if you continue to push yourself, you will eventually become the sort of person who embraces resistance. According to Pressfield, this is when you transition from pursuing your dreams as an amateur to becoming a professional. And once you begin to pursue your dreams like a professional, you will virtually guarantee your success.

9. The Law of Short Odds

Overnight success stories take a long time.

—Steve Jobs

The Law of Short Odds states that consistently pursuing low-risk opportunities with a reasonable payoff will bring greater long-term success than pursuing fewer high-risk opportunities.

I have a friend who makes his living betting on sports. Personally, I am not interested in betting on sports, but I do find it fascinating that people can make a decent living at it. In chatting with my friend, I have learned a fair bit about sports betting. At first, I was surprised to hear that successful sports betters don't count on long odds. Sure, sometimes they place bets that look like long odds. But they only do that if they've done their homework and they've determined that the odds shouldn't actually be as long as the sportsbook says. In reality, my friend told me, professional sports betters make their money by consistently making bets with smaller payouts. The reason why some bets have high payouts is because, if you bet on them, you are very unlikely to win. The odds are stacked against you. The greater your chance of winning, the lower the potential payout.

I've thought a lot about the lessons I learned about sports betting from my friend, and how they are applicable to many different areas of life. We all like the one-in-a-million success stories. We all like the story of the guy who supposedly "beat the odds" and made it big by mortgaging his house so he could start a business in his garage. We all love it when an athlete banks her future on making the team and she becomes a star, or when we hear about the guy who spent his last dollar at the racetrack and won big. We like those stories because we all love stories about longshots. We love to think that success is improbable.

But the path to success is almost never a longshot. Most people who sell everything to pursue a dream end up broke, just like most athletes get cut, and most people who bet on horses at the track lose. Instead, success is almost always a series of decisions that together make the outcome *less* of a longshot. Most successful people make a habit of playing short odds and doing so more often than you might think. It's no surprise that, according to the Internal Revenue Service of the United States, the average millionaire has at least seven different streams of income. For most millionaires, each of these seven streams is modest and low risk. But, when those modest wins are put together, they amount to a big payoff.

Now, the real secret in this law is this: you can shorten your odds on your own. I said above that successful sports betters don't usually bet on long odds, which is true. But the really successful ones find ways to create shorter odds because they know how to shorten the odds. Let me explain. A really good sports better will look at the odds being offered by a sportsbook and they will come up with their own odds. They will look at the game they are planning to bet on, and they will consider all the factors that might affect the outcome of the game. They will come up with a system where they assign numerical value to each of these factors, and they will eventually produce their own odds. This is called "handicapping." Then they take the odds they've created and they compare them with the odds offered by the sportsbook. And, if the sportsbook's odds are longer, the shrewd better knows that they should make that bet. According to the better in this situation, the sportsbook has listed something as having longer odds than it really has. This means they are offering a better payout than they should be offering. And so, it's not the longshot it appears to be to the untrained eye.

Now, making these "value bets," as they're called in the business, does not guarantee immediate success. You still have to do this many times to see substantial results. But, if your own handicapping system is accurate (and that can be a big if), you will eventually be successful.

Just like how sports betters shorten their own odds, people who are successful in all areas of life achieve success by shortening their odds as well. If I wanted to become a professional jazz musician, for example, I could always quit my job and move to New Orleans. But that would be a longshot. I don't know anything about jazz or jazz culture, and I'm not a very skilled musician. And I don't know anybody in New Orleans, either. But, if I devoted myself to becoming a skilled jazz musician, I would have just shortened my odds. It doesn't mean I will have automatic success. In fact, it would probably still be quite a longshot. But, now imagine that, in addition to becoming good at playing jazz, I also got to know some influential people in the industry. That would shorten my odds a little more. There are hundreds of other things I could do to shorten my odds even further. I could start releasing my music independently to build a following. I could offer to perform for free to try and build my reputation. I could visit New Orleans and introduce myself to every jazz musician in the city. In each case, the key question I would need to ask myself is whether making each decision would shorten my odds of succeeding or not. If you consistently work at shortening your odds, eventually you'll wake up one day and realize that what looked like a longshot before has now become a value bet. Once I have the skills, the connections, and the following, moving to New Orleans isn't nearly the longshot it once was, even if people don't realize that from the outside. People who don't know what I've been doing might say that I've taken a "leap of faith." They'll talk about how I dropped everything and took a huge risk. But that isn't true at all. Of course, there's still risk; there's always a chance it won't work out. But the point is that I would have significantly shortened the odds of success, making my move to New Orleans a bet worth making. Then, when I succeed, everyone will talk about my "lucky big break." But, in reality, no "big break" ever came. It was just a series of smart plays based on short-odds.

This is a law, which means, if you do this consistently in your own life as you pursue a goal, eventually you reach a tipping point where attaining your goal goes from being improbable to highly probable. You, too, can be an "overnight" success.

10. The Law of Infinite Feedback

While one person hesitates because he feels inferior, the other is busy making mistakes and becoming superior.

—Henry C. Link

The Law of Infinite Feedback states that success requires constant feedback. Successful people recognize that everything is feedback—absolutely everything. And it never ends.

When you sleep through your alarm, that's feedback telling you that you need to evaluate your sleeping habits. When you lose an important client, that's feedback that you might need to review your customer service practices. When you successfully finish running a marathon, that's feedback that your level of commitment and training was sufficient. When you gain a couple pounds, that's feedback that you need to have a look at your diet and exercise routines. When you get passed over for your dream job, that's feedback that there might be an area of your skillset or experience that you need to beef up. Any one of these experiences could have hundreds of feedback points. And successful people are constantly looking for them.

While this law is straightforward in principle, it is one of the most difficult laws for most people to follow. There's something inside each of us that resists following this law. We naturally want to celebrate our successes as proof that we are talented and special. And we want to forget about our failures as quickly as possible because they remind us that we might not be quite as talented as we like to believe. But thinking like this runs counter to the Law of Infinite Feedback and, therefore, prevents you from achieving success.

Learning to abide by the Law of Infinite Feedback requires a major paradigm shift: it requires you to separate yourself from your accomplishments and failures. The world-renowned Stanford psychology professor, Carol Dweck, wrote a famous book back in 2006 called *Mindset: The New Psychology of Success*. In this book she discusses this very process. Dweck is a leading scholar of achievement and success, and she is particularly concerned with the importance of mindset. In this book, she identifies two different mindsets: a fixed mindset and a growth mindset. People who have a fixed mindset tend to see their successes and failures wrapped up with their identity. When they fail at something, they feel like *they* have failed. People with this mindset tend to believe that things don't change. They believe that there are certain things they can't learn or do. As a result, people who have a fixed mindset will almost never experience true success because their mindset prevents them from doing what they need to do in order to have success.

People who have a growth mindset, on the other hand, tend to separate what they do from who they are. Whether they succeed or fail, they tend to derive their identity and self-worth from their effort, rather than their result. These people believe that intelligence and ability are not fixed. As a result, they have an underlying belief that they can learn to do anything, provided they put in the time and effort. They understand that effort always makes them stronger. Therefore, they tend to put in more effort than those with a fixed mindset, and, as a byproduct, they usually achieve more.

One of the experiments Dweck conducted in her study was with a group of ten-year-olds. She gave them a series of math problems that were intentionally more advanced than kids at that age could reasonably be expected to solve. She found that the children reacted in one of two ways: either they viewed these seemingly impossible problems as a welcomed challenge (even if they couldn't quite solve them); or they viewed them as a devastating revelation that they were not intelligent enough. The key difference between them was that the students with a growth mindset separated their identity and self-worth from the negative result they achieved, while the students with a fixed mindset saw their results as reflective of their self-worth.

Dweck describes the difference between these groups of children as the difference between embracing "the power of yet" and being subject to "the tyranny of now." The idea is that the students with a growth mindset concluded that they couldn't solve the math problems *yet*, but they assumed that one day they would develop the ability to pass the test, provided they studied hard enough. The other group of students, however, looked at their failure through the lens of *now*, with seemingly no sense of how they could develop their abilities in the future. If they couldn't solve it now, they felt as if this were a permanent situation. Not surprisingly, therefore, when Dweck asked the students what they would do next time to try and have more success, the students with the growth mindset said they would study for it, while many of the students with a fixed mindset said they would have to cheat.

Unfortunately, having a fixed mindset is not something we grow out of naturally. Those of us who have a fixed mindset as children will usually have a fixed mindset as adults as well. However, the good news is that it is possible to develop a growth mindset. It's also possible to improve your mindset further, even if you already have a growth mindset.

Dweck recommends something she calls "strategic praise" to help develop a growth mindset. We live in a culture that is results-based. Every bonus or grade or achievement award is based on results. This is not all bad. As you will see later on in this book, focusing on results is an important part of achieving success. But, in order to take advantage of the Law of Infinite Feedback, you need to focus on the process as well. You need to reward yourself for doing the right things, even if the results don't materialize the way you had hoped. When you work hard and do your best, make a strong strategic move, or exude honesty and integrity, give yourself a reward, even if you don't achieve your intended results. It can be as simple as buying yourself a chocolate bar or giving yourself a sticker. The point is that you need to start rewiring your brain to attach your identity to following the right process, rather than achieving specific results. Trust me, over time, this will work. You will find that you become increasingly detached from your old way of thinking and increasingly able to adopt a growth mindset.

Developing a growth mindset is a necessary part of following the Law of Infinite Feedback, because it gives you the ability to start to recognize feedback data points in your life. And the more you are able to develop a growth mindset, the more valuable the feedback you receive will be. Of course, it will be up to you what you do with that feedback.

Now, if you want to harness the power of this law, use it to your advantage, and accelerate your progress, you can take things to the next level. Instead of simply viewing things that happen to you as opportunities to receive feedback, you can begin to take a more proactive approach. You can adopt the approach of a scientist conducting experiments. By intentionally putting careful constraints on what you do, you can begin to get targeted feedback that you will be able to apply to very specific situations in your life.

For example, if you're looking for a new job, having a growth mindset and following the Law of Infinite Feedback means that every time you are rejected for a position, instead of being blinded by thinking that *you* have failed, you will be able to consider the various possible factors that led to your *application* being unsuccessful. This will, no doubt, yield some very important data, although it will be difficult to determine which factors ultimately led to your application being unsuccessful. However, if you want to harness the Law of Infinite Feedback and use it to take you to the next level, you could take a slightly different approach from the outset. Instead of sending out the same cover letter and resumé, with the same format, to every job, you might want to come up with a few different versions and see which one performs better. Then, take that feedback and tweak it for your next round of applications, if necessary.

You could run any number of similar experiments. You could decide to reach out by phone to half the companies you apply to, and not reach out to the other half; you could drop your application off in person to a certain percentage and email it to the rest; you could connect with a certain number of them on social media but not connect to the others. There are an almost infinite number of experiments you could run for something as small as applying for a job. The same thing could be said about virtually every area of your life.

The value of this approach is that it is much more targeted, and, as a result, it will bring you much more specific data. In the end, you will know exactly if connecting on social media or dropping your application off in person made any difference simply by observing which method leads to more interviews. Let's suppose, for example, you find that dropping off your application in person leads to interviews more often than sending your application in by email, but you also find that connecting with people from the company on social media makes no discernable difference. Once you've figured this out, you can incorporate dropping off your application as a rule going forward, and you can completely ignore social media. You will have just increased your chances of getting interviews at every future place you apply. And, if you continue to experiment by making additional tweaks to your process, you can continue to increase your chances again and again.

But taking this approach will require you to get comfortable with failure. By constantly testing all kinds of variations, you are increasing the likelihood that you will fail in the short-term in order to get the data you need to succeed in the long-term. If, for example, you want to find the best diet for your particular body and lifestyle, you could identify four different diet plans and try them each for two weeks. If you take careful notes about your experience each day, at the end of eight weeks you will have a wealth of data about each diet and how you respond to it. Then you can make a much more informed decision about which diet you adopt on a more permanent basis. You are accepting that you might have six weeks of failure before you find a diet that works.

But, once you find it, you'll know exactly which one is best for you long-term. This will put you ahead of 99.9% of people who ping-pong between diets every few months but claim that none of them work.

A lot of people mistakenly think that failure provides either more or better feedback than success. But this is not necessarily true. The reason why successful people talk about failure so much has to do with the fact that they have harnessed the power of the Law of Infinite Feedback by adopting a scientific mindset. As a result, they have experienced quite a bit of failure on their road to success. Failure is not more valuable for success, but it is useful because you can repeat it more often. Thomas Edison famously tried ten thousand different ways to invent the lightbulb before he succeeded. When he was asked about all these failures, he is reported as replying, "I did not fail ten thousand times; I simply learned ten thousand ways not to make a lightbulb." Albert Einstein was so convinced that failure was inevitable that he said, "Anyone who has never made a mistake has never tried anything new." And, Winston Churchill famously said: "Success is going from failure to failure with no loss of enthusiasm." In each of these instances, these men recognized that the shortest path to success—the path of the scientist—requires failure by design. While you still get feedback from your successes, in order to be able to fully harness the power of the Law of Infinite Feedback, you will need to use failure as a way to get feedback far more frequently. However, trust me when I tell you that every success will make up for a multitude of failures.

11. The Law of Clarity

If you don't know where you are going, any road will get you there.

—Lewis Carroll

The Law of Clarity states that success requires clarity of purpose. This means that you need to have a clear "what" and a clear "why." You have to know exactly *what* you're aiming at if you want to have any hope of hitting it. And you have to know exactly *why* you're aiming at it if you expect to overcome any adversity whatsoever. Both of these parts are necessary to have clarity of purpose.

Howard Hill is widely considered to be the greatest archer who has ever lived. He is the only man to have been inducted into three different halls of fame strictly for his ability with a bow and arrow, and he is also the only man to have won 196 field archery tournaments in a row. He set a new world flight record in 1928, and a new record for the heaviest bow ever used in 1932. He won multiple state titles, national titles, and, in 1943, he won the international field meet held in Milwaukee. He even wrote the first official set of archery rules in 1928. Everyone in the archery world knew him and marveled at his skill. In 1941, more than thirty-five thousand people gathered in Grant Park in Chicago to watch him. It was said that the crowd was so excited that they literally ripped the shirt off his back as they tried to get their hands on his arrows and quiver to keep as souvenirs.

There were many reasons why Hill was so famous. But, by far, the most impressive was his ability to hit a bullseye every single time. It was said that, not only could he hit a bullseye from fifty feet without fail, but that he could then split that first arrow with his second. The reason this is so impressive is because it requires a perfectly placed arrow. If he was off by even a quarter of a millimeter with his second arrow, he would not be able to split the first one. As Thomas Fuller has said, "A good archer is known not by his arrows but by his aim."

It's no wonder that everybody marveled at Hill's skill. His aim was impeccable.

The famous motivational speaker, Zig Ziglar, used to tell this story to his audience and then ask them whether they thought they could beat Howard Hill in an archery contest. Of course, the members of the audience would all shake their heads. There's no way an average person could ever beat the best archer in the world, right?

Well, Ziglar used to tell them, there *is* a way you could beat Hill. You would simply have to blindfold him so he doesn't know where the target is. It doesn't matter that he's possibly the most skilled archer to have ever lived. It doesn't matter that he has the perfect stance, that his hand is steady, and that his breathing is flawless. If he cannot see what he's aiming at, and if he doesn't know what direction the target is facing, he won't hit it.

Ziglar's point was simple but very important: if you do not have a clear sense of what you're aiming at, you cannot hit it, no matter how much you might try. You can acquire all the skills in the world, and you can practice from sunrise to sunset. Unless you can clearly see what you're aiming at, nothing will make a difference.

But that's what most of us are doing. Most of us don't have clear goals. Most of us aren't sure which direction we should be facing. Some of us don't even have a target set up. Denis Waitley put it like this: "The reason most people never reach their goals is that they don't define them."

You might think you're different. You might think you know what you want and why you want it. But, if your goal is even a little foggy—if it's not as clear to you as the letters on this page—you are still wearing your blindfold. If your goal is to have more free time, more money, less stress, a greater sense of purpose, a healthy relationship, or something along these lines, you are still wearing your blindfold. These goals are simply not clear enough. If you want to have more money, how much? What's the exact amount of money you want? When do you want to have it? Are you talking about income or net worth? How, exactly, will you be measuring your net worth? Why do you want to hit this specific number? What will it do for you in your life? Be *specific*. Focus on *details*.

Let's suppose, for example, that one of your goals is to have more free time to do the things you enjoy. A lot of people cite this as one of their goals.

I can tell you exactly how you can create eight hours of extra free time every day starting tomorrow. It's simple. Just quit your job. That would give you all the free time in the world.

Of course, you would probably tell me that you *can't* quit your job. After all, you need money to buy food.

Okay, then here's your new solution: quit your current job and get a part-time job instead. That will ensure that you have enough money to eat, and it will also give you more free time. Problem solved, right?

Again, you would probably tell me that you *can't* quit your job. You might actually like your job. You just want to have a bit more freedom in your life. Plus, you don't just want enough money to eat; you probably want enough money to maintain a certain lifestyle, too.

That's fine. But now you have a very different goal than you first started with. You don't actually want more free time; you want to earn more money while working fewer hours.

Do you see how that works? We just took a very general goal and made it more specific. In doing so, we gained a lot of clarity. In fact, we learned that the original goal was causing you to point your arrow in the wrong direction.

We could keep going like this for a while until the goal becomes so crystal clear that you can almost see it with your physical eyes. For example, we could figure out some possible avenues that might lead to you working less and making more. Maybe you could achieve this outcome by going back to school. Maybe you would need to switch industries. Maybe you would need to strike out on your own. Whatever you decide would be the best avenue for you to achieve your desired outcome, that can then become part of your goal itself. So, your goal wouldn't just be to earn more while working less. Your goal would be to earn $100,000 next year in a new position at XXX company working an average of XXX hours per month. That's a crystal clear goal. And that's the kind of clarity you need in order to have success. You need this level of clarity because it means everything you do in pursuit of your goal will have a very clear "what" and "why."

Having clarity about your *what* and your *why* go hand-in-hand. Think about it like this. When you get up for work in the morning, you probably have a very clear sense of what your immediate goals are and why you will pursue them. You get out of bed instead of hitting snooze; you have a shower and get dressed. Why do you do these things? Because they are *what* you need to do in order to be ready for work on time. And *why* do you need to be ready for work? Because you need to eat. It's very simple. Getting up and getting ready for work has a clear purpose. It has a clear *what* and a clear *why*, even if you're not consciously aware of them every single moment. And that's why most of us get up every day. Even on the days when we don't feel like rolling out of bed, we manage to do it. We might not always wear our best outfit, and there might be days where we skip our morning shower. But, more often than not, we manage to get ourselves to work.

If it's true that 80% of people don't like their jobs, how are they able to make it to work every day? It's because they have a clear purpose. They know exactly what they need to do and why they need to do it.

Now, once they get to work, it's a different story. For most people, there's a lot less clarity around what they're actually supposed to do at work and why. Just think about those things you *don't* get done while at the office. Chances are, if it's on your list and you don't do it, it's because you're lacking clarity about the what or the why. The same holds true for that woodworking project you haven't finished, that side hustle you've been thinking about but haven't started, or that friend you've been meaning to connect with. In each case, I'd be willing to bet that you're lacking a what or a why, or possibly both.

To have success, you need to be relentlessly focused on purpose. People who aren't successful are obsessed with the "how." But successful people know that the how doesn't matter that much. It's the "what" and "why" that matter. The famous German philosopher, Friedrich Nietzsche said, "a strong enough why can overcome any how." So, if you're worrying about the how, stop it. Make sure you have a what and a why. Then, you have clarity. The rest is all about mechanics, which can easily be learned.

12. The Law of Planning

If you fail to plan, you are planning to fail.

—Benjamin Franklin

T he Law of Planning states that careful preparation is essential for success. I have found that a lot of people underestimate the amount of time and effort they think they should devote to planning. For most people, if they would double, or even triple, the amount of time they spend planning, they could achieve their goals in less than half the time they expect it to take.

An unnamed woodsman was once asked, "What would you do if you had just five minutes to chop down a tree?" He answered, "I would spend the first two and a half minutes sharpening my axe." If you've ever tried to chop wood before you will know that a dull axe can be almost useless. If it's really dull, it's basically a big hammer. It would take at least three or four times as long to chop down a tree with a dull axe as it would with a sharp axe. So, by exercising just a little forethought, this woodsman knew that he would actually *save* time and energy by spending half his time preparing for his task properly. It might seem counter-intuitive, but if you stop and think about it, it makes sense.

Taking the time to properly prepare will allow you to execute much more effectively.

More recently, a newspaper column in Jefferson, Iowa, offered the following piece of advice: "Five minutes spent in sharpening the hoe, lawn mower, or even the shovel before work will save hours of time on the job, and the back won't be so lame the next day." Once again, the point is that taking time to prepare yourself and your tools to perform most efficiently will save you time and labor in the long run.

These are rather trivial examples that illustrate the importance of careful planning. But the reality is that, for most of us, the stakes are actually much higher than having to deal with a sore back the next day. For most of us, the difference between planning well and planning poorly can be the difference between living a life filled with meaning and living a life filled with regret.

Here's an extreme but powerful example of the importance of planning. Back in the early 1900s, two groups of explorers set out at the same time to Antarctica. Both groups had the same goal: to be the first people in human history to reach the South Pole. One group was led by the Norwegian explorer, Roald Amundsen. Even though he had already led many difficult expeditions, he knew that this trip would be especially treacherous. So, he began carefully planning the details for his trip in 1909, more than a year before he would set sail. He studied the methods of other experienced travelers, and he decided that, once his ship reached the shore of Antarctica, he and his men would transport all their equipment and supplies by dogsled. Again, because of the harsh winter terrain, he made sure to choose men for his team who were good skiers and dog handlers. And he ensured that they were all equipped with the best gear possible. He knew that, because he was using dogs to do most of the work, he would have to be careful to ensure they weren't overworked and had plenty of rest. Otherwise, the dogs would become too tired to complete the journey, both to the South Pole and back to the ship. So, he planned to travel for six hours every day. He calculated that this was enough time to travel twenty miles, while also allowing the dogs plenty of time to rest.

Amundsen and his crew of four other men set off from Norway in June of 1910. They spent seven months aboard their ship and reached Antarctica in January of 1911. The first thing they did was establish a camp where they landed. Because Amundsen had done such careful planning, he knew that he and the crew would not be able to carry enough supplies to last the four months it would take them to travel from their camp to the South Pole and back. So, before they set out on their journey, they spent seven months first setting up a series of supply depots along their route where they would have fresh supplies stocked and ready to pick up as they made their way to the South Pole.

All of Amundsen's careful planning eventually paid off. Despite the perilous nature of their journey, the worst hurdle they encountered was an infected tooth that needed to be pulled. On December 14, 1911, they became the first people ever to reach the South Pole. The journey was, by all accounts, a smashing success.

The second group of explorers who set out for the South Pole did not fare so well. This group was led by the British naval officer, Robert Falcon Scott. Scott had already done a little exploring in the Antarctic area, and so he felt confident that he was equipped to make the journey. But Scott didn't do nearly the amount of preparation Amundsen had done. As a result, he made some fatal errors. In the first place, instead of using dogs to travel to the South Pole, Scott decided to use a combination of ponies and motorized sleds. He reasoned that these would be faster and stronger, which is true. But he failed to recognize the harsh tole the weather would take on both the motors and the ponies. It took only five days into their trek before they were faced with their first major hurdle: their motors stopped working in the frigid temperatures. The ponies hardly fared any better. The crew ended up having to put all the ponies down just to save them from freezing to death. As a result, the men were forced to pull their 200-pound sleds themselves through the mountainous terrain.

Scott had not planned out the other aspects of their journey well enough either. The clothing the men wore wasn't warm enough, and each of the men ended up developing severe frostbite in the first few weeks. According to the diaries we have from the trip, it took one of the men more than an hour just to get his swollen feet into his boots each morning. Furthermore, because their goggles weren't of high enough quality, all the men developed snowblindness as well. Like Amundsen, Scott had established supply posts along his planned route. But Scott's calculations were off in almost every respect. His depots were not adequately stocked and were too far apart. In addition, they were not clearly marked, which meant that the men had to spend hours wandering around looking for them when their lives depended on the supplies they contained. As a result, he and his crew were constantly short on food. They were also short on fuel, which they used to melt snow so they could drink water. This led to severe dehydration. To make matters worse, Scott made a last-minute decision to take along a fifth man, even though all the plans for the trip were made based on a crew size of four men.

It took them ten weeks to travel the eight hundred miles from the coast to the South Pole. Once they arrived, they found a Norwegian flag flapping in the wind and a letter from Amundsen. Because of careful planning, the Norwegian team had beaten Scott and his team to the South Pole by more than a month.

As terrible as their trip to the South Pole was, this wasn't even the worst part of their journey. After finding that they had been beaten to the South Pole, they still needed to travel the eight hundred miles back to their ship. Along the way, Scott and his men were slowly starving to death and suffering from scurvy. Three of the men died early on during their trip back, which left Scott and one other crewmember to finish the trek to their camp. With about one hundred and fifty miles to go, Scott and the final crewmember realized they weren't going to make it. They sat down and spent their remaining hours writing in their journals, where they recorded the details of their journey. These journals are the only reason we know what they experienced.

Now, I realize that most of us probably aren't planning trips to the South Pole, but these two expeditions illustrate well the impact careful planning can have on your life. Unfortunately, too many people live their lives a lot more like Scott than Amundsen. Instead of actively taking control of their circumstances through careful planning, they are forced to react to the circumstances they find themselves in, which always becomes a fight for survival. They don't plan well, and so their lives are filled with set-backs, misery, and failure.

Most people react every day to the circumstances they find themselves in, rather than taking control of those circumstances by planning their day. They get up no earlier than they have to, their mornings are filled with activities that have to get done—getting dressed, brushing teeth, packing lunches. At work, they spend all day responding to colleagues, replying to clients, and reacting to crises. They don't plan out their workday. They don't stop to think about what the most efficient way would be to accomplish what they need to get done. They just sit down and start working on whatever someone else has put in their inbox. That's the equivalent of picking up the dull axe that happens to be sitting there and swinging it in hopes that the tree will eventually fall. It's no wonder that, by the time they get home and grab something quick to eat, they're mentally and physically drained.

It's no different when it comes to the bigger things in life. Most people want to be in a happy, high-functioning relationship, but they've given little thought to *how* they might work to attain this. They simply *hope* to meet the right person. Most people want to make more money, but, because they don't have a plan, the only way they will ever see a raise is if their boss walks up to them and hands them a cheque. Most people want to be in better shape, but, because they haven't made a plan, they never have enough time to work out or make a healthy meal. Most people end up spending their time constantly using the wrong tools, wandering around looking for supplies, and fighting to overcome the adversity that their own poor planning has created.

Whenever you find yourself reacting to your circumstances instead of taking control of them, that's a sure sign that you haven't spent enough time planning for success. Stop and think for a minute: How many tasks do plan out in your day? How many times do you stop to think what would be the most efficient way to get done what you need to do? How often do you sit down and plan you week, your month, or your year? Whether you have the biggest or

89

smallest goals in the world, it doesn't matter; if you don't have a plan, you won't be in control of your progress.

A good plan can be simple, or it can be complex. The amount of complexity will usually depend on what is required to accomplish your goal. But, no matter how simple or complex your plan is, every good plan will revolve around three key elements: there will be 1) a clear articulated outcome; 2) a recognition of the constraints you face and potential obstacles that might arise; and 3) a consideration of potential opportunities to enhance your level of efficiency. Each of these three elements will require different levels of detail or complexity, depending on your goal. Obviously, planning how to cut down a tree will require less complexity than planning an expedition to the South Pole. But both require a plan that includes these three elements.

The reality is that things will almost never go exactly according to your plan, no matter how good your plan is. But that's not the point. Dwight Eisenhower once said, "In preparing for battle I have always found that plans are useless, but planning is indispensable." Planning is indispensable because it gives you direction. It gives you clarity about which actions you should take and when. It provides markers by which you can measure your progress. And it forces you to prepare for potential obstacles that might have otherwise derailed you completely. But, most importantly, planning gives you control. It allows you to take initiative, and so it allows you to determine exactly how and when you will reach your goal. When you plan well, everything you do will look a lot more like Amundsen's expedition than the expedition of Scott. And that's a good thing.

So, what's your plan for success?

13. The Law of the Master and the Grandmaster

Passion is the side effect of mastery.

—Cal Newport

The Law of the Master and the Grandmaster states that you must be very good at something in order to have success, but you do not need to be the best of the best. According to this law, there are two paths to success: you can be among the top 10% or among the top 1% of all the people in your field. Those who are in the top 10% are masters of their craft because they are substantially better than the vast majority of their peers. Those who are among the top 1% are the grandmasters of their field because they are the best of the best. According to this law, you must be either a master or a grandmaster in order to achieve success.

However, while both paths—that of the master and that of the grandmaster—can lead to incredible success, the path of the master will lead to greater success more often than the path of the grandmaster. This might seem counterintuitive because we've been conditioned to believe that being the grandmaster is always better than being the master. But, in reality, the majority of successful people have become successful by intentionally becoming masters, rather than grandmasters.

In 2004, and then again in 2008, Hazel Tindall was crowned the fastest knitter in the world, clocking in at two hundred and sixty-two stitches in a three-minute span. If you know anything about knitting, you'll know that that's quite impressive. Hazel would almost certainly be among the top 1% of knitters in the world. And her skill has allowed her to start a blog, sell her knitting patterns, write multiple books, and even star in two films about knitting. By all accounts, Hazel has become a grandmaster knitter.

But, of course, Hazel didn't learn to knit overnight. Becoming the fastest knitter in the world was a journey that took her well over sixty years. In fact, she claims that she can't even remember a time in her life when she didn't know how to knit.

It is quite common for people like Hazel to spend a lot of time practicing their craft. To become the best of the best at almost anything, you need to put in a lot of time and concentrated effort. After all, becoming the best is a competition. Not only do you have to improve, but you have to improve at a faster rate than everyone else. That's not an easy thing to do.

Take basketball, for example. Basketball is one of the fastest growing sports around the world. It is estimated that roughly 450 million people play basketball on at least a semi-competitive basis. Of those 450 million people, about seventy thousand are good enough to play at a professional level in one of the many leagues around the world. And, out of those seventy thousand people, only five hundred and twenty-nine players are good enough to play in the NBA, which is widely considered to be the best basketball league in the world. This means that fewer than one in six-thousand basketball players are good enough to play professionally in some capacity. And for every player in the NBA, there are nearly one million inferior basketball players across the globe. Statistically speaking, to play in the NBA you would need to be better at playing basketball than virtually every other person in the world. It's no surprise that, for most professional basketball players, basketball has been their whole life ever since they were little kids.

Just like with Hazel Tindall or professional basketball players, people who are the grandmasters in their field will likely achieve success. But the problem is that it's incredibly difficult and time-consuming to become the best of the best. The path of the grandmaster has a very high cost, and there's no guaranteed return.

Now, most people recognize that being among the top 1% in their field will mean substantial success. In your case, being among the top 1% might not mean that you can play basketball professionally, but it might mean that you get a nice promotion, salary increase, or that any number of doors that were previously locked are suddenly swung wide open for you.

Unfortunately, however, most people, whether they realize it or not, assume that being in the top 1% is the *only* way to truly succeed. But that is not true. Here's the reality: *being among the top 10% will often open up more opportunities for you to succeed than being among the top 1%.* This is because the amount of time you need to dedicate to your craft in order to be among the top 10% in the world is a fraction of the time needed to become among the top 1%. Roughly speaking, about 25% of the skills needed in any domain will put you in the top 10%. So, to become among the top 10% in the world at playing hockey, for example, you will need to learn how to skate, shoot, and pass reasonably well. But, if you want to be among the top 1%, you will need to go way beyond the basics. You will need to spend hours perfecting your backhand and become highly proficient at using the edges of your skates. You will need to work on "reading" the play so you can react a fraction of a second faster than your competition, and you will need to use targeted dryland training to make sure that you are stronger than your opponent in every situation. So, while it might be daunting to think of becoming the best hockey player in the world, becoming among the top 10% is a much more attainable goal.

And here's the rub: it takes about twice as much time and effort to go from being in the top 10% to being the top 1% as it does to get into the top 10% in the first place. Have a look at this chart below. It represents the typical development curve when it comes to developing a skill. As you can see, when you first start practicing a skill, you need to put in a bit of effort without seeing significant results. But, as long as you continue putting in the effort, all of the sudden you'll find that you become very good very quickly. As long as you've continued to put in the effort, you can usually be among the top 10% at this point. But notice what happens after that. Going from the top 10% to the top 1% takes a lot more effort and happens a lot more gradually.

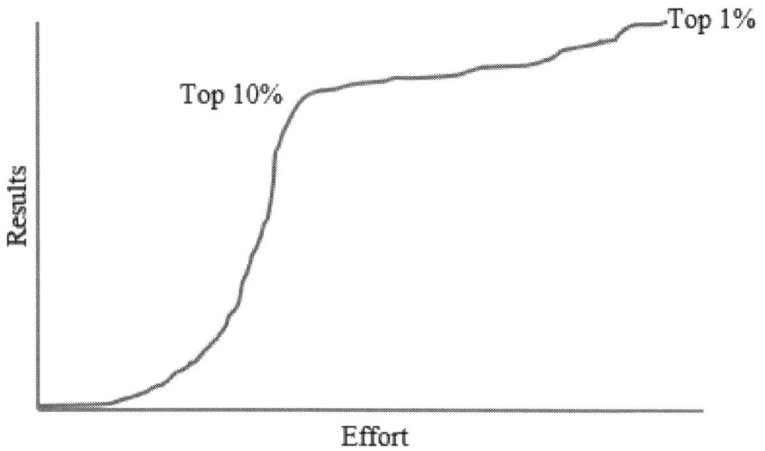

Because it takes disproportionately less time to become among the top 10% than it does to become among the top 1% in almost any field, taking the path of the master is more beneficial because it allows you to take advantage of other avenues of success as well. To become the best knitter in the world, the best basketball player in the world, or the best hockey player in the world takes an incredible amount of dedication and practice. It means that you probably won't be able to go to law school or start a business, at least not until you achieve your goal. But by becoming among the top 10% in your field, you will be able to pursue these other avenues of potential success. In the end, you might not have the opportunity to play in the NBA or NHL, but you could get into broadcasting, scouting, coaching, managing, or training, and there are probably thousands of other possibilities you could pursue based on the combination of your knowledge of the game and other skills you were able to develop.

To compound things, in many fields, the difference between being in the top 1% and being in the top 10% is virtually unnoticeable. In fact, this law exposes a secret almost nobody wants to acknowledge: 90% of the world would never be able to tell the difference between someone in the top 10% and the top 1% in most fields. My sister, for example, is an excellent pianist. She's been playing her whole life, and she is probably among the top 10% of all piano players in the world. I am amazed at how good she is. But she has a friend who is much better. He is very close to being among the top 1% of all pianists in the world. Now, I know a little about music, but I'm not very good at playing the piano. When I hear my sister's friend play, he sounds just as good as my sister. You see, she can hear the difference because she knows all the little nuances of the craft. But, to me, the average person, they both sound great.

This is important to realize because it is probably true in your particular field as well. Hardly anybody could tell the difference between a salesperson in the top 1% and a salesperson in the top 10%. Practically nobody would be able to distinguish between a parent who is among the top 10% and a parent who is among the top 1%. We all know when we've encountered a bad salesperson or when we see a bad parent. But, the difference between the top 10% and the top 1% is not noticeable for most people. Someone who is among the top 10% of all salespeople is still a really good salesperson. They would still earn promotions and receive incredible opportunities because most people would see them as being among the best in their field. When you combine the information from the chart above with the fact that almost nobody can tell the difference between someone in the top 10% and someone in the top 1% in most fields, you can begin to see that being in the top 1% is not as important as you might have previously thought. The investment just might not be worth the payoff.

Of course, if you are working on a skill that you particularly enjoy, you can always continue to try to become among the very best in the world. There's no law against that. But, for most of the skills you have, you would be best off becoming among the top 10%. Just think, you could become in the top 10% in two different fields in the same amount of time it takes someone to become among the top 1% in a single field. Becoming highly proficient in multiple things is how you can harness the power of this law and use it for your advantage. Most successful people are good at multiple things. They have chosen to become a master in multiple domains, rather than to become a grandmaster in one domain.

So, unless you have the dream of making it to the Olympics, or you have a burning passion to become the very best in the world at a particular thing, the Law of the Master and the Grandmaster dictates that becoming among the top 10% will usually transform your effort into success more effectively and efficiently than becoming among the top 1%.

14. The Law of Done

The best is the enemy of the good.

—Voltaire

T he Law of Done states that done is always better than not done. Therefore, to have success, you need to constantly focus your attention and energy on getting things *done*. A lot of the brightest people I've worked with over the years struggle with this law because they fill their to-do lists with things that make their projects *better* but don't necessarily bring those projects any closer to being *done*. It's a subtle difference, but it's incredibly important.

Winston Churchill famously said, "perfection is the enemy of progress." Personally, I like the way Voltaire put it better: "The best is the enemy of the good." But, in the end, they're both right. You see, unless you get things *done*, they will never bring the results you hope for. Nobody dreams of writing half a novel. But how many half-finished novels are tucked away in drawers or buried on hard drives across the globe? Probably millions. Most aspiring novelists spend more time hoping it will be good than working to get it done. No matter how good you might think your half-finished novel is, if it isn't done it doesn't matter. The difference

100

between professional writers and those who dream of being professional writers is that professional writers get their writing projects done. That's it. Most writers will write terrible first novels. But those who go on to have success will finish the terrible first novel, learn some lessons, and move on to the next one. And that next one just might not be as terrible as the first one.

We like to call people who are constantly trying to make things better "perfectionists." But I don't think that's always the most helpful term. First of all, most people I know who violate the Law of Done aren't trying to make their projects perfect; they're just trying to make them a little better.

Another reason why "perfectionist" doesn't quite capture the full extent of this law is that when we call someone a perfectionist the implication is often that they will never finish. After all, pretty well anything could be made just a little bit more perfect. But you can violate this law and still finish your projects. Any time you spend more time than is absolutely necessary on a project, you have almost certainly begun to violate the Law of Done. To be sure, every report could be made a little bit nicer. But, adding that extra font or changing the way the tables are laid out doesn't get the report any closer to done. And so, it is a waste of time. The problem is simply that devoting time and energy to things that won't get your projects any closer to being finished is a waste of time

Now, it's important to note that there will always be a certain quality standard you must meet. But successful people recognize that these standards are included in the definition of "done." So, for instance, a novel needs to be thoroughly edited and proofread to make sure it's readable. Based on what I've said above, you might be tempted to think that those tasks are not essential because they don't help get the novel finished. But that's not quite right. The right way to look at it would be to say that getting the novel done *includes* these tasks. So they are necessary. But each of these tasks should be broken down further. What are the essential actions you would need to take to get the editing and proofreading done? You would need to determine what these actions are and then make sure to focus solely on them in order to get the editing and proofreading *done*.

The key at every point is that you must decide at the outset the exact level of quality that needs to be included to get your project done. If you're writing a report that requires you to include a complex chart, then every minute you spend working on that chart is well spent because it's helping to get the project done. But if your report doesn't demand the chart, every second you spend working on the chart is wasted time. Always remember: *just because you're doing something doesn't mean you're getting something done.*

Somewhat counterintuitively, the way to work along with the Law of Done is to focus your attention on progress, not the end result. Let me explain. If you spend your time thinking about all the things your novel could bring— notoriety, freedom from your job, a new identity as a writer—you end up teaching your brain to focus on writing the novel that will bring all of this. Your brain is very sophisticated. If you tell it that your novel needs to allow you to leave your day job, your brain will begin to focus its attention on making this happen. This is a really cool thing. But the problem is that your brain knows your novel can't be average, if you want it to support you. So it pushes you to look for ways to make it a little bit better.

At first, this might seem like a good thing. I mean, who doesn't want to do their best to achieve their dreams? But the problem is that writing a best-selling novel will almost never happen to first-time writers. Your path to success will be much quicker and more direct if you write a bad first novel. Everything you learn in the process will make your second novel better. And what you learn in that process will make your third novel better. And so on.

Following the Law of Done does not mean that you do a bad job; it simply means that you stop focusing on making your project better. Every action you take needs to contribute to getting it *done*. As soon as making it better becomes your focus, you violate the Law of Done and actually work against your own success. However, when you consistently focus on the actions that will bring your various projects to completion and challenge yourself every time you feel the urge to do something that will not get you closer to done, you will fast-track your path to success.

15. The Law of Momentum

An object in motion will stay in motion unless acted upon by an outside force.

—Isaac Newton

The Law of Momentum states that the more successes you have the bigger your successes will be. Another way to put it would be to say that little success breeds big success.

Many of us work against this law by pursuing massive goals without breaking them down into smaller chunks. We decide, for example, that we'll lose fifty pounds this year. That's a perfectly fine goal. In fact, I'm a big believer in setting massive goals. But the thing about setting massive goals is that you will almost certainly fail unless you figure out a way to create some momentum. So, if you set the massive goal of losing fifty pounds in a year, you might want to start by setting the smaller goal of losing one pound in a week. Losing fifty pounds seems impossible. But losing one pound is certainly do-able. And, once you have success, you will be more motivated to do it again. And, once you do it again, you'll be more motivated for the next week. And, once that momentum carries you through a week, you will be motivated to keep going. Eventually, losing two pounds in a week will be do-able. And, before you know it, you will have lost fifty pounds.

If you've ever followed an exercise routine, you will have experienced the power of momentum firsthand. You will know that it's much easier to get up and go to the gym if you've already done it three days in a row than it is after two days off. Why is it harder for most people to get up and go to work on Monday than it is on Tuesday or Wednesday? The answer is simple: on Tuesday and Wednesday you have momentum.

The Law of Momentum is at work in every area of our lives. If you want success, you need to be aware of it, stop working against it, and start working along with it instead.

You can do this in a few different ways. But the way that I recommend most often is by allowing yourself to win. I'm not sure why, but we seem to have an inbuilt resistance to letting ourselves win. We all like to win. But we don't like to let people win, and we don't like it when people let us win. It doesn't feel right. There's something deep inside that makes us believe victories should be earned, not given. But sometimes we need to get comfortable with letting ourselves win in the short-term so we can earn the victory in the long term.

Let me give you an example of how this works from my own life. For many years of my life I was a night owl. Ever since I was a teenager, I would stay up until the wee hours of the morning and sleep in as late as possible. I always thought that I was wired that way. Eventually, of course, I had to get up early every day for work. And then I started reading about how most productive people seem to get up early. So, I decided to give it a try. At this point, I was getting up pretty regularly at 7:30. So, I began setting my alarm for

7:15. Just fifteen minutes earlier. I knew that if I started trying to get up at 5:00 I wouldn't be able to keep it up. So I made sure I set a target that I knew I could hit. When I managed to get up at 7:15 for a couple of weeks, I felt really good about myself. I felt like I had won. So, I decided to try getting up at 7:00. Because I was used to getting up at 7:15 at that point, getting up fifteen minutes earlier wasn't a big deal. And, again, when I managed to get up consistently at 7:00, I felt really good. I could even see my productivity starting to increase, which was really motivating. So, I harnessed this momentum and, two weeks later, I started setting my alarm for 6:30. I had gained enough momentum at this point that I could make the challenge a little bigger. Instead of getting up fifteen minutes earlier, I could get up thirty minutes earlier. And it went well. Once again, I succeeded. At this point, I felt unstoppable. I was getting up early every day, getting more done than I ever had before. So I moved up my alarm time again, this time to 6:00. A few weeks later, I changed to 5:30, then 5:00. And eventually I was getting up at 4:00 a.m. every day for a year. There's no way I would have ever been able to start getting up at 4:00 a.m. unless I built up the momentum first.

Sometimes the initial goal you need to set will be so small that it might seem silly. For example, I had a friend who was working from home and was having trouble getting into her day on Monday morning. She had a family and, after a hectic weekend with her kids, she found that she was slow getting into the swing of the week. She hated this because it made her feel behind most of the week. When she told me this, we talked about this law. I explained to her that she was creating negative momentum, which was staying with her through the week. I suggested that she reverse this by doing something very simple: I told her to do one small task for work on Sunday night before going to bed. It could be that she simply opened her work email and took a look at what she had to respond to in the morning. Or she could spend five minutes working on a project. It didn't matter what it was, she just had to do something work related before going to bed. The point was not for her to get anything done; the point was to create the smallest bit of momentum before she started her workweek so it would be easier for her to keep it rolling on Monday morning.

After a few weeks, she reported back to me that this had transformed her Mondays and her whole week. This was all because she started abiding by the Law of Momentum.

So where can you use the Law of Momentum to your advantage in your life?

16. The Law of Rocky

The good news—for you—is that most people in life quit. So, staying in the game is half the battle and puts you light years ahead of others.

—Robert Kiyosaki

The Law of Rocky states that success is only possible for those who survive the game. Everybody knows that success is about achieving something. But few of us stop to realize that, many times, success is simply a matter of staying in the game long enough to win. A lot of times, the difference between those who succeed and those who don't is that those who succeed stay in the fight longer than those who fail.

Success can be a lot like boxing. One of the ways you can win at boxing is by outlasting your opponent. This was the calling card of Sylvester Stallone's wildly popular character, Rocky Balboa. At one point, when Rocky is speaking with his son, trying to impress on him the importance of staying in the fight, he says: "It ain't about how hard you hit. It's about how hard you can get hit and keep moving forward; how much you can take and keep moving forward. That's how winning is done!" This quote epitomizes Rocky's entire fictitious career. In each of the Rocky movies, Rocky would win his fights by taking a beating and never giving up. When other fighters would stay on the mat, Rocky would take blow after blow, only to stagger back up to his feet time and time again. Eventually, his opponent would get tired of swinging, and Rocky would start to turn the tide of the fight. In the end, he would win because he could outlast his opponents.

This law is at work more than you might think. For example, during the 2002 Olympic Games in Salt Lake City, the Australian speedskater, Steven Bradbury, won one of the most unexpected gold medals in Olympic history simply by following the Law of Rocky. Bradbury was competing in the men's short track one-thousand-meter event. He won his first heat convincingly, meaning that he advanced to the quarterfinals, where he was up against two gold-medal favorites, Marc Gagnon from Canada and Apolo Anton Ohno from the US. Only the top two racers from his heat would advance to the semi-finals, so Bradbury knew he was in tough from the beginning. He skated as fast as he could, but he couldn't keep up with the other two skaters and wound up finishing the race in third place, just missing the opportunity to advance—or so he thought. It turns out that, after the race, it was determined that Marc Gagnon was disqualified, thus bumping Bradbury into the semifinals. If he hadn't skated his tail off to make sure he finished in third place, even though he knew only the top two skaters would advance, he wouldn't have been able to take advantage of the opportunity to advance.

In the semi-finals, it was a similar story. He was, once again, competing against heavy favorites from South Korea, China, and Canada. He knew before the race even began that he probably wouldn't be able to beat the others outright, so his strategy heading into the race was to try and stay as close to these other skaters as possible. That way he would be in a position to take advantage of any mistakes they might make. And, once the race began it was clear that he would have a difficult time doing even that. But, when all of the three other favorites crashed on the last lap, Bradbury was in the perfect position to sail past them and qualify for the finals. Once again, by staying in the fight Bradbury positioned himself to be able to take advantage of the opportunity to win when it presented itself.

From the first lap of the gold medal race, it was clear that, of the five skaters in the race, Bradbury was the weakest. He was in last place the entire time. The skaters from South Korea, Canada, America and China were all jockeying for position, while Bradbury was doing everything he could just to keep from falling out of sight. This went on for almost nine laps. But, as the skaters rounded the last corner and saw the finish line in sight, the four powerful skaters each saw their opportunity to win and pushed hard to establish their position. The Chinese skater was shoulder-to-shoulder with the American skater, and he lost his balance, taking him out of the race. The Korean skater and the American skater then leaned on each other, causing both of them to tumble to the ice and tripping the Canadian skater in the process. Just like that, the top four skaters all went sliding into the boards in a heap, once again leaving Bradbury all alone to sail across the finish line untouched and win gold.

After his gold medal win, Bradbury readily admitted that he didn't win because he was the fastest skater during the race. Instead, he said that, to him, the medal represented all the hard work he had put in for the prior decade that prepared him to take advantage of the opportunity in the moment. Bradbury was smart. He knew that he would never win if he tried to jockey for position with the other, superior skaters. So he shifted his focus. Instead of trying to win by being the fastest, he tried to win by lasting the longest. He relied on all his hard work over ten years of training to keep him in the race long enough to be ready for an opportunity. He admitted that he had talked with his coach about the possibility that the other four racers would push themselves too hard and maybe even crash. So, when he saw them start to go down, he was prepared to use every last ounce of energy to get himself across the finish line before they could recover.

Just like Bradbury, we will all encounter times where we need to shift our focus from winning to surviving in order to have success. Your path to success does not necessarily require you to be the biggest, fastest, or smartest. But it does require you to survive.

However, because you're likely not going to be competing in the Olympics any time soon, let me explain in practical terms what survival means for most of us in our daily lives. For most of us, survival means iteration. So many people I speak to talk about getting their "big break." They're looking for that job that will solve their financial problems, or they're waiting for their business to "catch on." Sometimes they're trying to manufacture an event that will bring them closer to their kids, or they're hunting for that one sale that will put them over the top. Whatever their problem, a lot of people make the mistake of thinking there is a single solution or a magic bullet.

But a single solution will almost never work. And magic bullets don't exist. No successful artist makes enough money to live off a single painting, at least not at first. Those who do make a living do so by making a little money off multiple paintings. Similarly, very few authors will write a massively successful best-seller on their first try. Most successful authors have written dozens of books that all sell reasonably well. Or again, few relationships are mended by a single gesture. It usually requires multiple gestures before a broken relationship can be repaired. Even business people rarely have a single business that succeeds. They usually have a number of businesses, each one contributing to their bottom line. In other words, success in every area of life requires iteration.

Iteration is important because it keeps you in the game. If a business person loses one stream of income, they have at least six others still flowing in. If an author writes a book that doesn't sell very well, they have others that are still selling, which means they can continue to write another book. Relationships that are based on multiple interactions at different levels will not be completely severed if one of those levels of interaction changes. Iterating allows you to stay in the game longer, which naturally means that you are in the position to take advantage of opportunities when they arise. Those opportunities might look like a "big break," but they aren't.

So, if you want to harness the power of the Law of Rocky, the first thing you need to do is figure out how you can iterate.

17. The Law of Bamboo

Success requires both urgency and patience. Be urgent about making the effort, and patient about seeing the results.
—Ralph Marston

The Law of Bamboo states that the speed of results is proportionate to the quality of roots. I have already mentioned when discussing the Law of the Master and the Grandmaster that the usual success curve looks something like this:

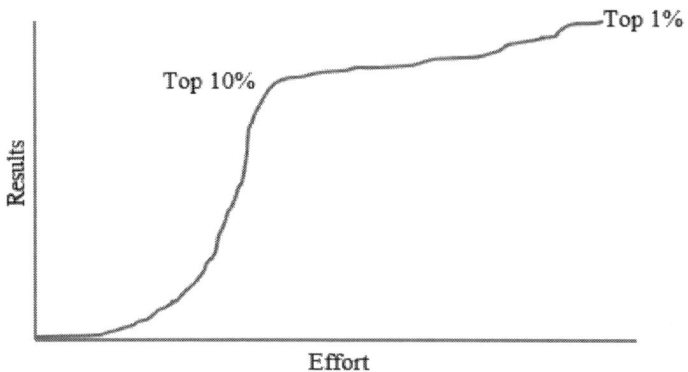

When I showed you this chart back in that chapter, I focused on the top part of the chart, how the effort required to go from among the top 10% to the top 1% means that it isn't always worth it to become the best of the best in a specific field.

But here in this chapter I want to focus on the bottom of the chart. The fact is that, no matter what you pursue, there will always be some time at the beginning where your efforts don't appear to be paying off at all. This is the point at which many people lose steam and even give up. Some people will keep putting in the work all the way until the curve is about to go straight up before deciding to throw in the towel. I can't tell you how many times I've seen someone put in a bunch of work and then decide to give up right before their results are about to start pouring in.

When I meet somebody about to give up at this point, I will usually try to encourage them to stay the course by explaining the Law of Bamboo. As the motivational speaker, Les Brown, likes to point out, achieving success is a lot like growing a Chinese bamboo tree. You see, when you plant a Chinese bamboo tree, you have to water it and fertilize it for five years before it ever breaks out of the ground. That's a long time to care for a tree that you can't see.

Just imagine for a minute how often you would be tempted to give up on that tree during those five years. There are going to be days during those five years when you doubt whether the tree will sprout at all. It would be tough to force yourself to go out and care for it on those days, but you have to do it if you want the end result. Imagine what your neighbors would say when they see you caring for a patch of mud every day. They would probably question your sanity. Perhaps they would try to convince you to give up.

The reason the Chinese bamboo tree takes five years to sprout is because it's putting all its energy into setting up an incredible root system. It's setting up the root system that will support the tree and ensure it remains healthy when it is fully grown. Even though we might know this, it's hard to feel motivated when we don't *see* results.

But, if you can continue caring for the tree for five years, at some point during that fifth year, the tree will grow a staggering ninety feet tall in only six weeks. This means that if you planted a hybrid poplar (which is one of the fastest growing trees) at the same time as a Chinese bamboo tree, after five years the poplar could be nearly forty feet tall, while the bamboo has yet to break the surface of the ground. But, if you were to check on them six weeks later, you would find that the bamboo was more than twice as tall as the poplar.

Whenever I see someone give up just before they're about to take-off, I tell them that giving up would be like deciding to give up on your Chinese bamboo tree three weeks before it was about to sprout. Imagine if you spent five years caring for this bamboo seed and waiting for it to sprout. But, after waiting for so long, you decide to cut your losses and move on. So you leave. What an incredible loss. You would have spent five years caring for something that you never get to enjoy.

Well, that's the way most people treat success. They work hard at something for a little while and then give up. But there is a curve to success that most people simply don't know about. Like with bamboo, there will always be a period at the beginning when your effort seems to be yielding no results. The hardest part is that it *is* always possible that your bamboo tree has died. That means you will have been caring for it for nothing. And there's no way to know that unless you keep caring for it for the full five years.

In the case of the bamboo, the plant is building a very strong root system underground. So there is growth, you just can't see it. The same is true when it comes to success. You are growing. You are putting habits and practices in place that will pay long-term dividends, but only if you see it through. You will only realize the value of the root system once you see the plant sprouting.

However, here is where the previous law—the law of iteration—intersects with the law of the bamboo. You see, the wise thing to do is to plant two or three, or five or ten, different bamboo seeds. If you're going out to water it every day anyway, you might as well water all of them at the same time. And, if one or two don't take for some reason, you still have a handful of others that have.

So, what's your Chinese bamboo tree?

18. The Law of "No"

The difference between successful people and really successful people is that really successful people say no to almost everything.

—Warren Buffett

The Law of "No" states that success requires saying "no" more often than saying "yes." We are all bombarded with opportunities every single day, whether we recognize them or not. You might think that the reason people fail to achieve success is because they do not seize these opportunities. But the real reason people fail is not because they say "no" to opportunities; it's because they say "yes" too easily to the wrong opportunities. Based on the wisdom he found in the Bhagavad Gita, Robert Brault has recognized this very point and has summarized it well: "We are kept from our goal, not by obstacles, but by a clear path to a lesser goal." Most of us are constantly distracted from accomplishing anything great because we are busy pursuing opportunities to do things that are mediocre.

This insight has given birth to a practice known as keeping an avoidance list. An avoidance list is simply a list of things you will avoid at all costs because they distract you from accomplishing your most important goal. The idea is that you should keep this list in a place where you can see it regularly to remind yourself of all the lesser goals you will not pursue under any circumstance in order to keep your focus squarely on the things that will bring you success.

The reason why this practice is effective for so many people is because the lesser goals that threaten to distract us are very rarely obvious. In fact, they are usually things that are only slightly less important than our main goals.

There's a well-known, apocryphal story purported to be about a pilot named Mike Flint that illustrates this law well. Flint, so the story goes, was an excellent pilot. He used to fly U.S. presidents around in Air Force One, and he eventually became Warren Buffett's private pilot. One day, after working for Buffett for ten years, Flint and Buffett had a conversation about Flint's career ambitions. While he enjoyed his job, Flint told Buffett that he wanted to do something more than simply fly his boss around in a private jet.

According to this story, Buffett offered Flint some advice. First, he told Flint to write down his top twenty-five professional goals. These were to be the twenty-five things Flint most wanted to accomplish in his career. Once Flint had made the list, Buffett told him to look over his list and circle the five goals he cared most about. When he had finished, Buffett told him to take a good look at the twenty goals that were not circled and declared that the path forward for Flint was now set: the five goals he circled should be the things he spends all his time pursuing, and the twenty he didn't circle would become the goals he must avoid at any cost. Buffett explained that the remaining twenty items will be the things that constantly try to prevent Flint from having success by pulling his attention away from the five things he cared most about. Every time Flint would try to make progress on one of his top five goals, he would have to also actively say "no" to the other twenty items on the list. Otherwise, his focus would be divided and he wouldn't achieve anything.

While we now know that Buffett never actually gave Flint this advice, the story nevertheless illustrates a critical basic point: the lesser goals you will constantly have to say "no" to will be goals that you actually want to accomplish. As David Allen says, "you can do anything, but not everything." You might want to be the best parent in the world, a successful entrepreneur, an Olympic swimmer, and a champion bug collector. But you almost certainly will not be able to do all of these things—at least not at the same time. If you don't decide which goal you will focus on, you will end up constantly shifting your focus between them, and you will, ultimately, not achieve any of them.

Even if, for example, you decide that being the best parent in the world is your primary goal, if you do not actively practice saying "no" to the other goals, they will secretly creep in and prevent you from becoming the best parent you could be. You will have bad days. You will have days where you don't *feel* like being a good parent. On those days, you might be tempted to take a break from your kids to meet up with your swim team or head outside and look for bugs. The next day, you will almost certainly feel the tug to do it again. And, before you know it, you're pursuing your bug collecting dream at the expense of your primary goal.

Or, again, if you don't actively say "no" to your goal of being an entrepreneur, you will almost certainly face conflicts as you try to focus on being the best parent in the world and also run a business. You will, no doubt, have meetings that cut into play time with your kids, urgent problems that prevent you from making them the healthiest meals, and business questions that distract your attention even when you're physically present with them.

The point is that the "lesser goals" you have to say "no" to will not necessarily be lesser in an obvious sense. They are only lesser because you've decided that they aren't the most important things to you. This makes them tricky to deal with. It's pretty easy to justify staying at the office late three days a week to build your business because that will help you accomplish a valuable goal. But, if your primary goal is to be the best parent in the world, spending extra time away from your family might actually be holding you back from accomplishing that more important goal.

We all have a long list of things that we want to pursue but would actually prevent us from making progress on things that are more important based on our own standard of success. Sometimes this has to do with big things like your career or general life direction. Other times it has to do with smaller things. It doesn't matter; the principle is the same. Just think about it for a minute. Have you ever started something just to run into obstacles? Maybe you've started a side hustle or a hobby. What happens after the initial excitement of your new venture wears off? It gets tough. And what does your brain do? It starts telling you that maybe you should shift your focus. Instead of pushing on with your side-hustle, your brain says maybe you should learn to play the guitar. And that sounds good. It never suggests something you're *not* interested in. And that's the trouble. What happens after the initial excitement of learning the guitar wears off and it starts to feel hard? Your brain suggests something else. Maybe you should finally master that new recipe you've been planning to work on. And so you stop practicing guitar and you dive into your new cooking adventure. And on it goes.

We all do this about one thing or another in our lives. Sometimes it might be obvious, and sometimes it might be really subtle. And the problem is that each thing you pursue could be a legitimate goal. The thing is that, by not saying "no" to all of your "lesser goals," you will almost certainly never achieve success. Your side-hustle will never get off the ground. You won't know how to play the guitar, and you will never actually learn to cook. If you had just remained focused on one of these things and said "no" to the others, you would have achieved something.

So, if you want to have success, compiling your own avoidance list is a must, even if it is only in your head. What are the things in your life that you would love to pursue but don't align with your central goals? Spend some time figuring this out and then start saying "no" to them consistently.

19. The Law of "Yes"

> Everything in the world began with a yes. One molecule said yes to another molecule and life was born.
>
> —Clarice Lispector

The Law of "Yes" states that success requires constant adaptability to changing circumstances. People like to say that the only constant in life is change. And this is true. But many of us don't thrive amid change. In my experience, I have found that this is especially true for people who care about productivity and success. We tend to be the kind of people who like routine and systems. We like to find a formula that works and then use that formula day in and day out.

This is especially true when we face problems or challenges. Our immediate reaction is often to see how we can "fix" things. By "fix," we usually mean "make things like they used to be when everything was working just fine." But approaching change in this way will lead you to violate the law of "yes."

There's an old rule in improvisational theater referred to as the "yes, and" rule. According to this rule, whenever you are improvising with other people you should always build on what your fellow improvisors do and say. Because everything that happens is improvised, it's very important that everyone involved works to keep the flow going. If you watch improv at all, you'll know that there are some pretty strange things that can happen. But if one of the improvisors disagrees with something being said, the flow is immediately interrupted.

Imagine you are watching an improv group perform a scene about Christmas morning. Everything is moving along as you might expect. Characters are pretending to open gifts, and there's some witty banter being delivered back-and-forth. But, all of the sudden, in the middle of the scene, one of the improvisors pretends to point out the window and exclaims, "Look, the aliens are coming!" At that moment, all the other improvisors have a choice to make. They can either dismiss the comment by explaining it away and carrying on with their scene as it was. Or they can accept this new piece of information and build on it. The rule of "yes, and" means that the other improvisors must choose the latter; they must pretend to also see the aliens and then build on that scene. They should never say, "no, those aren't aliens; those are just bright streetlights." If they did say this, they would immediately kill the flow of the scene. Instead, they should all pretend to see the aliens and build the scene further. They might run for cover or look for weapons, or they could think of some other way to build on the scene. There are literally thousands of different things they could do to build on what has just been said. No matter what the other improvisors choose to do, they all know that the rule of "yes, and" demands that they continue to build the scene. Otherwise, the entire scene gets killed.

The Law of "Yes" is a lot like the improv rule of "yes, and." To live in accordance with the Law of "Yes" means that you accept circumstances as they are. You don't pretend things are better or worse than they really are. And you don't try and fight change when it happens. When your business has a dip in sales, you don't immediately try to explain it away or pretend it didn't happen. You don't get anxious that you're going to fail at life. You accept it and look forward. When a friend lets you down, you don't waste time and energy venting about it to your partner. You don't spend time wondering how this could have happened to you. You simply take this new information into consideration and move forward. Maybe this means you distance yourself from this friend, or maybe you decide to forgive them. Either way, you accept what happened and you adjust accordingly, always looking forward. You don't interrupt your flow.

When you commit to following the law of "yes," you will find that all kinds of opportunities open up for you. Just like how the improv rule of "yes, and" opens up thousands of new directions the improvisors can choose to go, so also, every time something happens in your life that forces you to adjust, there are new opportunities just waiting for you to take advantage of them.

20. The Law of the Black Swan

Only those who risk going too far can possibly find out
how far they can go.

—T.S. Eliot

The Law of the Black Swan states that new
possibilities emerge as you explore new territory.
Thousands of years ago, people commonly referred
to impossible events as black swans. At that point, nobody
had ever seen a black swan, so, naturally, it was presumed
that all swans were white. Back then, to say that something
was a black swan was a way of saying that it was impossible.
However, in 1697, a group of Dutch explorers became the
first Europeans to see actual black swans in western
Australia. From that point on, the term took on a different
meaning. No longer did it refer to something that was
impossible; after black swans were discovered in real life,
the phrase came to refer to something that was thought to be
impossible but was later proven to be possible.

That's a good lesson for all of us. We all have black
swans in our lives. We all have things that look impossible
for us today. And many of those things very well might be
impossible right now. For a lot of people, it's virtually

impossible to double their income, learn a new language, or patch up broken relationships. It's impossible in their current situation because there's no obvious path they can take to get where they want to go. And in the face of impossibility, most people either give up or never start at all.

But, here's a powerful secret: *every single time you take action in your life you create new possibilities*. The explorers who found the black swans did not set out to look for black swans. They were actually on a rescue mission, looking for a crew of fellow explorers who had disappeared some time earlier. While out on this mission, they discovered many interesting things about Australia, one of which was the existence of black swans. If they hadn't set out on a rescue mission, they would have never discovered the black swans.

The important lesson is that new possibilities emerge when you take action, even if you're taking action on something else. My friend, Ian, is a great example of how this works. Ian went through a tough time. He lost his job as a financial strategist and was having trouble figuring out what he should do. He had been in the finance industry for more than a decade, and he had worked his way up from the bottom. When he lost his job, he was exclusively managing million-dollar clients and routinely travelling across the globe. After he lost his job, he spent a few weeks feeling sorry for himself and waiting for his phone to ring with another job offer. It never came. He reached out to some of his contacts to see if there was a job out there, but it was a tough time for the economy. No one was hiring.

One day he decided to take action. He decided that doing *something* was better than doing nothing. So he took a job at a small consulting firm. He was overqualified for this job, but he took it anyway. After a few months, he was attending a meeting where a client mentioned that they wanted some strategic advice about a business opportunity. Ian offered some thoughts. He didn't think anything of it. But two weeks later this same client phoned Ian to tell him that his advice had just made the man very wealthy. He offered Ian a job on the spot to manage the new business he had acquired. This was different than anything Ian had ever done before, but it sounded like an interesting opportunity, so he took it.

Not long after that, Ian met some colleagues at a manager's conference. He hit it off with them immediately, and over the next few years their friendship grew. Eventually this new group of friends decided to strike out on their own. They started their own firm. Ian now gets to bring together his expertise in the financial world, the consulting world, and the business world. And he loves it. Ten years ago, becoming a business owner would have been the furthest thing from his mind. He would have thought it was impossible. And, back then, it probably was. But today, it's his dream job.

Ian's story is a good illustration of what it means to follow the Law of the Black Swan. By taking action—any action—opportunities will arise that turn impossibilities into possibilities. In Ian's case, he was in a place where he thought the highlights of his career were all behind him. He never thought he would ever again be able to do the kinds of things he did in his old job. When he took action, he wasn't planning on getting his old job back; he knew he would never have that opportunity again. But simply by taking action, new opportunities came up. If he hadn't taken the job at the small firm, he would never have met the client who offered him a management job. If he hadn't taken that management job, he would never have met the colleagues he eventually started his business with. If he hadn't gained experience as a manager and consultant, he would not have had the necessary skills to start his own business.

Just like how the Dutch explorers would never have found black swans if they hadn't embarked on their rescue mission, so Ian wouldn't have become a business owner if he hadn't taken that initial job at a local consulting firm. By taking action, things that were impossible became possible.

The lesson here is to take action. Do *something*. Never let yourself do nothing. If you do nothing, things that seem impossible for you today will be impossible for you tomorrow. But, because doing something can lead to all kinds of possibilities—possibilities you might never have dreamed of—exploring new territory is the best way to make today's impossibilities possible for you tomorrow.

21. The Law of Focus

Concentrate all your thoughts upon the work in hand.
The sun's rays do not burn until brought to a focus.
—Alexander Graham Bell

The Law of Focus states that success requires focused attention. Simply put, you cannot have success at something if you do not pay any attention to it. And the more you focus on it, the more likely your success will be. If I never focus on playing the guitar, for example, I will never learn how to play it. But the more I focus on learning how to play, the more likely it will be that I become good at playing the guitar.

Master motivator, Tony Robbins, puts it this way: "Where focus goes, energy flows." And he's right. If you give your attention to problems that cannot be fixed, or to skills that don't help you accomplish your goals, you will begin moving toward those things in your life, rather than the things you actually want. Your focus is like your steering wheel. Whatever you spend your time focused on is where you will direct your energy. And where you direct your energy determines the direction you will begin to move in your life.

If you spend twelve hours a day focused on video games, for example, you will become good at playing video games. But you probably won't be very good at much else. If you spend all your time thinking about how your friend stabbed you in the back, you will become resentful. If you spend a lot of time focused on how you would have handled that difficult conversation differently, you will probably come up with some great, useless alternatives. And if you focus mostly on what other people have and what you don't have, you will become jealous.

On the flipside, if you spend time thinking about how you can help those in need or how you can build healthy relationships, or how you can build your net worth, you will find that you are more fulfilled, and that success comes more easily in virtually every area of your life.

So, what do you spend your time thinking about? Do you spend your time thinking about that movie you watched last night? Do you spend your time thinking about how your best friend hurt you last year? Do you spend your time thinking about how unfair it is that your co-worker is getting a promotion? Do you spend your time thinking about some useless argument happening on social media? Or do you spend your time looking into the future, focused on what you can do to help others and what steps you need to take to reach your goals?

If you spend your time thinking about useless things from the past, your brain will use its energy up on these things. Thinking about how your mother said something mean to you causes you to imagine various scenarios where you confront her. It works you up emotionally. You might not realize it, but in those moments your brain is preparing you to deal with the problem you're focused on. The same is true when you think about the movie you watched last night.

You imagine what you would have done if you were faced with the challenge the main character faced. You might question why the director made certain choices. You think about what you would have liked to see done differently. And so on. Once again, by allowing your brain to use its precious energy trying to solve problems that don't really matter, you are turning your steering wheel away from the direction you really want to go. Naturally, you will find yourself off course.

Even trying to focus your attention on what you want by telling yourself *not* to focus on something else won't work. It's easy to fall into the trap of telling yourself *not* to think about failure or resentment. But, even though you don't mean to, you will be sending your brain a signal to focus on these things. If I tell you not to think about an orange pig, what immediately comes to mind? An orange pig, of course. You see, our brains will focus on whatever we think about— even if we're trying to tell ourselves *not* to think of it.

That's why the only way to harness the power of this law is to focus your attention on what you want in your life and away from the things you don't want. If you don't want toxic relationships in your life, stop thinking about the ones you've had in the past, and start thinking about the positive relationships you'll have in the future. If you don't want to be broke, stop thinking about the little money you have, and focus on what you can do to increase your income. The way to work along with the Law of Focus is to remain resolutely focused on exactly what you want in your life, and to banish the things you don't want from your mind.

There are two core strategies that will help you transform your focus. The first strategy is what I call exercising thought captivity. It works like this: when you find yourself thinking about how difficult it is to work with a particular colleague, for example, catch yourself and turn your attention immediately to something positive by coming up with three things you can do to rectify the situation. You could buy them coffee when you see them next week; you could start working with your office door closed; or you could look for a new job. These could be good ideas or bad ideas. It doesn't matter. The point is that you need to start developing patterns of thinking that work with the Law of Focus instead of against it. If you follow this exercise every time your mind slips into thinking about something negative or useless, you will become more successful because you will find that your actions almost miraculously start taking you in exactly the right direction. Whenever something happens that threatens to pull your attention away, force yourself to steer your attention back to what you want.

The second strategy that will help you keep control of your focus is also extremely powerful: write down your goals. Make sure you're as specific as possible, and be sure to review them every single day when you get up and before you go to bed. Force yourself to keep them in the front of your mind. By continuing to keep them at the top of mind, you will find it much easier to focus on them. In fact, over time you will find that all kinds of things you encounter in your day cause you to focus on them. Instead of being reminded of useless things from your past, the movies you watch, people you observe, and the restaurants you visit will all start triggering thoughts about your future. Everything you encounter will begin to work along with you, helping you reach your goals.

Following the Law of Focus is one of the ways you can make success feel effortless in your life. If you really master this law, it will feel like the universe is conspiring to bring you success. And that's a game changer

22. The Law of Solutions

The major difference between successful and
unsuccessful people is that the former look for
problems to resolve, whereas the latter make every
attempt to avoid them.

—Grant Cardone

The Law of Solutions states that success is proportionate to the number or significance of problems solved. Every successful person has either solved a lot of small problems or a few big problems. Either way, their success is determined by how well they've solved those problems.

There is nothing on earth more valuable than a solution to a problem. We face hundreds of problems every single day. And virtually every product or convenience we enjoy today is the result of someone coming up with a solution to a problem. Most jobs are just a series of problems that need to be solved. Some problems are bigger than others. Some are more urgent, and some are less urgent. We value people who help us solve problems in our lives, and they value us when we can help them solve problems in their lives. We live in a problem-solution world.

All of the great advancements in our world can be boiled down to solutions to problems. For example, do you know why Josephine Cochrane invented the first automatic dishwasher in 1893? It was because her maid kept breaking her dishes when she washed them. Josephine had a problem, and the dishwasher was her solution. Do you know why Ole Evinrude invented the first outboard motor in 1906? It was because he was trying to row two miles to bring an ice cream cone to a girl he liked, and, by the time he arrived, the ice cream had melted. He had a problem, and he knew that, if he could find a way to make his boat go faster, he would have a solution. Do you know why Alexander Graham Bell invented the telephone in 1875? It was because he was searching for a way to help deaf people communicate. He had success because he saw a problem and worked to solve it. No matter what kind of success you have in mind, whether or not you achieve it will come down to how well you are able to solve problems.

Once you know the importance of solving problems, you'll be able to see how adopting a solution mindset can shortcut your path to success. In every situation, you should learn to identify problems and potential solutions. If you provide solutions to your boss's problems, she will value you more highly. If you solve problems for your customers, they will buy from you and be happy with your product. If you help your friends solve their problems, they will like you more. This is true of every aspect of life. If you solve problems for people, you will find success.

There is one note of caution, however: most of the time people's problems are not what they appear. Sometimes they will even be unaware of the problems they have. There's an old saying in sales that you sell people what they want and give them what they need. If you sell someone an expensive sportscar that they can't afford, they will eventually resent you for taking advantage of them. You might have made the sale, but you will probably lose the customer. On the other hand, if a customer comes in looking for a sportscar but you find out that they really can't afford one, you should do whatever you can to get them in a sportscar within their budget. You sell them what they want (a sportscar), but you give them what they need (an affordable payment). Not only will you make the sale, but you will likely have a much happier customer. When they are looking for another car at some point in the future, they are far more likely to come back and see you.

In that little scenario I just painted, who do you think was the more successful salesperson over the long term, the one who sold the customer a sportscar they couldn't afford or the one who sold the customer what they wanted while also giving them what they needed? The answer, obviously, is the latter.

Once you know about the Law of Solutions, you can apply it to virtually every area of life. Your friend might tell you that they want to go out dancing, but they might really need someone to talk to about a rough patch they're going through. If you train yourself to look for problems and solutions, you will recognize this. So, you will know to choose a place where you can give them what they want (dancing) but also what they need (a quiet corner where you can talk about the thing they're going through). Similarly, when your elderly parent or grandparent falls ill, they might tell you that they want you to leave them alone, even though you know they need care. If you recognize that the real problem is that they feel like they're losing their independence, you can rearrange things in their home to make it easier for them to do all the basic things they need to do on their own. Once again, you're giving them what they want (independence) and also what they need (care). When you follow this law over time, you will eventually become quite good at recognizing problems and potential solutions. And once you start to recognize them, you will find them everywhere.

As I have already mentioned, you can harness the power of this law in two ways in order to shorten the time it takes you to achieve success: you can either increase the size of the problems you solve, or you can increase the number of problems you solve. As I write this, Elon Musk is currently trying to solve some big problems to do with the sustainability of life here on earth. That's why he's trying to colonize Mars. It's a set of massively large problems he's trying to solve. As a result, if he succeeds, that success will secure his place in history textbooks for generations to come. But there are plenty of smaller problems, too. For example, every fast-food joint is attempting to solve a lot of smaller problems. Everyone needs to eat, and it can be a hassle to make every meal at home. So, they provide a quick fix. It's a solution to a problem. The problems fast-food restaurants are solving aren't nearly as big as the ones Elon Musk is trying to solve. But that's okay. It just means that, in order to have success, fast-food restaurants have to solve this problem for more people.

When you follow the Law of Solutions, the path to success is straightforward. No matter if you ultimately choose to solve one big problem or many smaller problems, the first step is the same: solve *a* problem. Because success is a matter of finding solutions to problems, in order to take a step toward success today, you need to identify a problem for which you can find a solution. So, what's the problem you are going to solve today?

23. The Law of Causes

Maybe you are searching among the branches for what only appears in the roots.

—Rumi

The Law of Causes states that success requires constant examination of causes, not symptoms. One of the differences between people who find success and people who don't is that average people focus on symptoms, while successful people focus on causes.

Imagine the following scenario. A man rushes into the hospital complaining of extreme back pain. The doctor takes one look at him and immediately realizes that there's a giant knife lodged deep into the man's back. The man begs the doctor to give him something for the pain because it hurts so bad. So the doctor prescribes some heavy painkillers and sends the man home. Once the painkillers kick in, the man's pain subsides and he feels much better. He considers the problem solved.

But, of course, the problem isn't solved. The painkillers help with the symptom (pain), but they don't do anything about the cause (the knife). It will only be a matter of time before the pain returns and the man needs another prescription.

Now imagine another scenario. A woman gets a job selling cars. She has never had a sales job before, so there is a steep learning curve. At first, she isn't very good. She goes a long time without selling anything. She watches as her co-workers make sale after sale, but she can't seem to close a deal. She tries everything she can think of to become better at sales. But nothing seems to work. One day, one of her colleagues jokes that the secret to his success is that he eats Wheaties every morning. The woman hears this at figures she might as well try it. So, that night she goes out and buys her very first box of Wheaties. The next morning, she gets up and has herself a big bowl. And, wouldn't you know it, that day she sells ten cars.

She assumes it was the Wheaties that made the difference. After all, it was the only thing she changed from her routine.

But, of course, the difference was not really the Wheaties. The Wheaties were just a symptom of something much more important. Her success was really the result of her determination to improve as a salesperson, and all the hard work she put in during the weeks when she couldn't sell a thing. The fact that she was willing to try anything—including eating Wheaties—was a symptom of that determination.

I tell you these two silly stories to illustrate a very important point: *to have success, you need to become obsessed with finding the causes for all the symptoms you observe in your life, both good and bad*. Failing to recognize the causes of negative symptoms will mean that you never get rid of the problem. Like the man with a knife in his back, your treatment of the symptoms will only last so long.

Eventually those symptoms will return. The only solution is to treat the problem causing the symptoms.

In a similar way, failing to recognize the true causes of positive symptoms is also a problem because it will prevent you from ever replicating your success. The woman who attributed her success with selling cars to eating Wheaties in the morning will be surprised when she continues to eat Wheaties each morning but doesn't ever see the same success again. The point is that, if you mistake symptoms for causes of your success, whatever success you manage to achieve will never last long.

The Law of Causes is a law that we all know intuitively. We all know that it would be silly to treat a knife wound with painkillers or a band-aid. We all know that eating Wheaties won't magically make someone a good salesperson. We all know the fights we have with our loved ones are usually about something other than the thing we're fighting about. And we all know that the promotion you received at work isn't really because you're a "good guy."

Oscar Wilde's well-known book, *The Picture of Dorian Gray*, tells the story of a young, innocent man named Dorian who gets caught up in a life of pleasure and power after falling in with a particularly sordid crowd. Dorian's new friends admire his youthful innocence, and one of the friends has a portrait of Dorian painted in an attempt to capture his youth and innocence forever. Dorian's friends tell him that it's a shame that youth is fleeting and that he will soon not look like the innocent boy in the portrait. Worried that his most impressive characteristic will be lost as he ages, Dorian curses the portrait, believing that it will only remind him of everything he will soon lose. He flippantly says that he would give his soul if only he could remain like the portrait, and if the portrait could age instead of him.

Over time, Dorian falls deeper and deeper into a life of pleasure and debauchery. Before long, Dorian realizes that something strange is happening: as he becomes more and more cruel to those around him, the portrait is changing. His wish has come true; instead of his face bearing the marks of the sordid life he leads, his sins are being recorded on the canvas. So he hides the portrait in a room upstairs and carries on.

Eighteen years pass, during which Dorian becomes widely known as a cruel, scandalous man. But, because he continues to appear so youthful and innocent, people in polite London society continue to accept him among their ranks. However, after murdering one of his friends and blackmailing another to dispose of the body, Dorian is overcome with guilt. He decides that he cannot continue to live this way, and so he determines to get rid of his secret once and for all. He takes a knife up to the room where the portrait lays hidden and uncovers it. It shows an old, distorted man so filled with wickedness that he can hardly stand to look at it. In a fit of rage over what he had become, Dorian stabs the painting over and over. Other people in the house who were downstairs hear a terrible crash coming from the room, and so they rush in to find the portrait in pristine condition, showing Dorian in his original, youthful form. On the floor lies the body of an old man, horribly wrinkled and disfigured, with a knife plunged into his heart.

This story is a good illustration of the dangers of treating symptoms instead of causes. The underlying principle throughout the book is that, as the soul is disfigured by one's lack of character, these disfigurations are revealed on the body. Everything Dorian did throughout his life that was evil and wicked would slowly take away his youthful innocence. Dorian was concerned about losing his youthful face, but instead of treating the root cause of the problem—namely, his character—he treats the symptom. He manages to keep his youthful face without addressing the real problem.

But this is always a recipe for disaster. Failing to address the root cause of problems will always come back to bite you, as it did for Dorian. In the end, who he became tore him apart on the inside, and eventually killed him.

I'm willing to bet that you probably don't have a magical portrait of yourself in your attic, like Dorian did. But, I'm also willing to bet that there are some things in your life that you have tried to solve by treating the symptoms instead of the cause. I know this because we all need to be reminded of this law constantly.

But the fact that the Law of Causes is a *law* means that you will never escape it. No matter the area of your life, if you treat the symptoms instead of the causes, you will not achieve much. If there's a problem that crops up in your business, relationships, or in your character, you will not achieve the level of success you could achieve without first dealing with the cause of the problem.

So, if you're serious about achieving success, you must commit to relentlessly pursuing the causes of all the symptoms in your life.

24. The Law of Multiplication

The greatest shortcoming of the human race is our
inability to understand the exponential function.
                              —Albert Allen Bartlett

The Law of Multiplication states that success requires
exponential growth. There is growth by addition and
there is growth by multiplication. To have true
success, you need to train your brain to think in
multiplication, not addition.

Let me explain how this works by telling the stories of
two different people that I know. First, I will share with you
the story of my friend, James. When I met James, he was
making $50,000 per year. He had dreams of increasing his
salary to $100,000. One day, he decided to take action and
make this dream a reality. So, he set up a meeting with his
boss to discuss a salary adjustment. After a brief
conversation, he was pleasantly surprised to hear his boss
agree to give him an extra $2,500 per year. So, for the next
year he made $52,500. He was happy that he added $2,500
to his salary, but he still had a long way to go to hit his goal
of $100,000. So, the next year he decided he needed to take
action again. James had a friend who has just started a

landscaping business, and he decided to see if he could pick up some hours with his friend for some extra cash. His friend agreed to take him on to work on the weekends, and James was ecstatic. He figured out that, if he worked every weekend, in addition to his regular workweek, he could add an extra $15,000 each year to his salary. And he did just that. So, for the next year he made $67,500. James was happy. In two years he managed to raise his yearly income from $50,000 to $67,500.

But James had a problem: he was running out of time. Sure, he added an extra $17,500 to his yearly income, but he was practically working every single day of the week. There was no way for him to add more to his bottom line unless he could magically manufacture more time. So, he decided to make a change. He began looking for a new job that would pay him a higher salary. It took him a year of searching to find something that was a perfect fit. But, eventually his patience paid off, and he found a job that would pay him $80,000 per year. Once again, he was ecstatic. The only downside was that this new job required him to work some weekends, which meant he couldn't help his friend with his landscaping business anymore. But, because he was increasing his yearly salary from $67,500 to $80,000, James thought it was a no-brainer to take the job. After all, he would be making more money *and* have most of his weekends off. It was a win-win.

On top of everything, the new job James landed had some great performance incentives. So he knew that, if he put in the time, he would be able to cross the $100,000 threshold within ten years. James worked his tail off and, seven years later, he finally hit his goal.

Most of us would probably look at James's story and praise him for his resourcefulness. He was clearly committed to earning more money, and he found ways to do it. It's true; he was resourceful. He managed to double his salary and hit his income goal in ten years of hard work and incremental change. He has nothing to be ashamed of.

However, consider Rachel's story as an alternative. Rachel also started off making $50,000 per year and had aspirations of making $100,000. But, instead of having an addition mindset, Rachel had a multiplication mindset. So, when she thought about achieving her goal, she didn't think about how she could add incrementally to her income here and there. She thought about how she could find a way to multiply her income. And so she did her research based on this mindset, which means that, while James was calling his friend about taking on some hours at his landscaping business, Rachel was thinking about a whole different range of options. She figured out relatively quickly that working part-time for a friend or relying on a small salary increase wouldn't give her the results she was looking for, so she explored more options until she found the solution that would work for her. She had done her research, and she determined that starting her own online business would be the best way for her to reach her goal. She knew it would be a lot of work, but it was the best way she could multiply her income. At first, it was just a side hustle, something she spent a few hours a week on. It took her a while to make any money, but she knew that, as long as she kept at it, she would eventually earn a lot more than she was currently making at her job.

And she sure did. Her first year she made about $10,000, which isn't bad at all. But by the end of her second year, she had already made and extra $50,000. She had hit her target of doubling her income in two years! And, because she maintained a multiplication mindset, she set out in her third year to double her income again. So, she made some adjustments and, by the end of the year she was making $100,000 from her side hustle alone.

As she continued to make more and more money with her business, she began looking for additional opportunities to multiply her income. Again, she wasn't interested in adding a few dollars here and there; she wanted to pursue opportunities that could, over time, multiply her investment. So, after doing some research, she started investing in the stock market and in real estate. Instead of doubling her income, pretty soon Rachel was tripling her income every single year. Ten years later, when James was finally hitting his goal of $100,000, Rachel had just achieved economic independence. She had enough money coming in from her investments each year that all of her expenses were covered and she wouldn't have to "work" again for the rest of her life.

Both James and Rachel worked very hard. Both were smart. Both were capable of accomplishing whatever they set their minds to. And both eventually accomplished their initial goal of earning $100,000. But Rachel accomplished this goal in just two years, while James took ten. And, as she reached her goal, Rachel continued to multiply her income. In the end, Rachel's financial success was in a different stratosphere from James's success. The difference comes down to a simple difference in mindset: James had an addition mindset and Rachel had a multiplication mindset.

When you understand the Law of Multiplication, your mindset changes. The way you think about problems changes, and so the solutions you come up with change as well. In the two stories I have just told you, Rachel's path didn't have immediate returns. For someone with an addition mindset, that can be tough to evaluate. How can making nothing for months bring you closer to your goal of making more money? With a multiplication mindset, however, the equation makes sense.

If you want to apply the Law of Multiplication to your life, begin by asking yourself honestly how you are being held back by not following the Law of Multiplication. Maybe you're holding yourself back in terms of your finances, like James did. Or, maybe you're restricting your emotional health or the quality of your relationships. Maybe, for you, it's all of the above or something else entirely. It doesn't matter. If you pick just one area of your life and commit to following the Law of Multiplication in that area, you will begin to see success.

25. The Law of Daily Decisions

Life is a matter of choices, and every choice you make makes you.

—John C. Maxwell

T he Law of Daily Decisions states that the little decisions you make consistently each day are more important than the big decisions you make in life. When successful people talk about their success, they often point to the big moments in their lives where "everything changed." Big life events, such as losing a job, having a child, or moving to a new country can serve as catalysts for a transformation in anyone's life. In those moments, we often make commitments to achieving success. And those are important moments. But, successful people know they aren't the *most* important moments.

I remember when I bought my first house. It was a big decision because it was, by far, the biggest financial commitment I had made to that point in my life. But it was also a statement to myself and the world that I was entering a new phase in life—a phase where I was going to settle down and settle into life as a homeowner. When I look back, I remember the moment I decided to make an offer on the house. I remember it because it was an important moment for me. But I don't remember all the little decisions that made that one big decision possible. I don't remember deciding every month to pay my bills on time for ten years leading to that moment. I don't remember deciding not to eat out hundreds of times so I could add a few extra dollars to my savings account. I don't remember deciding that I didn't need designer clothes or a new car. I don't remember all the times I made the decision to go to bed early so I could perform well in my job the next day.

But each of these seemingly insignificant decisions made the big decision possible. Paying my bills on time for years improved my credit score, which allowed me to be approved for a mortgage. Deciding not to spend my money on take-out, new vehicles, or expensive clothes allowed me to save up enough for a down payment faster. All the times I got up early for work led to increases in my salary. This increased the amount of money I could save for my down payment and also increased my household income so I would be approved for a larger mortgage. There were probably thousands of other small decisions I made that ended up making the big decision to buy a house possible.

It's pretty easy to see how small decisions about money over time can lead to a big decision like buying a house. But this same principle is at work in every area of life. The small decisions to make healthy choices when it comes to your diet and exercise will make it possible for you to run that marathon or have the swimsuit body you've always wanted. The small decisions to read about personal development for fifteen minutes every day will help to put you in the right mindset so you can better take advantage of opportunities that cross your path. The small decisions you make hundreds, or even thousands, of times each day determine what you think about and how you behave. These decisions will prepare your brain to pursue success.

But where this law gets really exciting is when you begin to see all your decisions come together. My daily decisions about money prepared me to be financially ready to buy a house. But, my daily decisions to work hard and learn as much as possible during the year I spent doing home renovations as a teenager helped to give me the knowledge and confidence I needed to make a wise purchase. My daily decisions to work on my own personal development for years helped to put me in a place where I knew I was ready for the stability of homeownership. The small decisions I made in various areas of my life all had some impact on that big decision.

This is always the case. All the small decisions you make today, tomorrow, next week, and next month will impact all your big decisions. Every little decision you make today—even those decisions you won't remember tomorrow—will have an impact on who you are and what you are able to do in the future. You will never be able to predict how this is going to work in advance, but it's part of the Law of Daily Decisions, so you can be confident that it will work.

When you truly recognize how all your daily decisions contribute to every step you take toward success, your entire mindset will be transformed. Making the small decision to eat a healthy breakfast not only helps your waistline, but it will also help you maintain energy throughout your day. This, in turn, will improve your productivity. And who knows what that might lead to. Making this small decision will also help to build the important power of self-discipline, which can grow and become the key to anything you could possibly want. The small decision to eat a healthy breakfast, when made consistently, can literally transform your life.

On the flipside, choosing to eat an unhealthy breakfast will have the opposite effect. You will feel sluggish later in the day, and so your performance will decline. You will put on weight, which will lead to health problems down the line. And you will weaken your ability to exercise self-discipline, which means the next time you are faced with a decision, you will be more likely to make another self-destructive choice. The small decisions you make each and every day can transform your life positively. But they can also transform your life negatively.

Now, just think: every single decision you make has this same power. Whether you decide to read or watch TV, that decision will change your life. Whether you decide to go to bed or stay up late, that decision will change your life. Whether you decide to forgive or harbor resentment, that decision will change your life. Whether you decide to invest your money, spend it, or give it away, that decision will change your life. We all make thousands of little decisions every day that have life-changing potential. Once you see your daily decisions in this light, you can see how the quote from John Maxwell at the beginning of this chapter is literally true: "Life is a matter of choices, and every choice you make makes you."

26. The Law of Expansion

To achieve great things, two things are needed: a plan and not quite enough time.

—Leonard Bernstein

The Law of Expansion, which is also known as Parkinson's Law, states that every task will expand to fill the amount of time allotted for it. The recognition of this law dates back to 1955, when Cyril Northcote Parkinson published a humorous essay in *The Economist* in which he made a curious observation: the number of people employed in the British Civil Service *increased* at precisely the time the British Empire was imploding and the amount of work needing to be done was *decreasing*. In his essay, Parkinson was pointing out that bureaucratic growth is not proportionate to the amount of work needed to be done. If there are more people doing less work, the implication must be that each person is working slower and, therefore, getting less done.

In recent years, Parkinson's observation has been picked up and applied more generally to time management. If more people could be busy all day doing less work, the implication of Parkinson's observation is that the more time one is allowed to complete a task, the longer it will take to complete that task.

Numerous studies conducted in recent years have confirmed this conclusion. For example, in a study focused on employees working at customer service centers, it was found that these employees used as much time as they were given to respond to customer queries, regardless of whether those queries required simple or complex responses.

In this study, researchers gave half the employees a time-limit of ten minutes and the other half a time-limit of ten seconds to deal with each customer query. Surprisingly, they found that there was no discernable difference in the quality of service provided by either group, despite the fact that those who were given ten seconds to respond accomplished more than sixty times what those who were given ten minutes accomplished. Whether they were given ten minutes or ten seconds, the employees used the time they were given to accomplish the same tasks with the same level of effectiveness. The conclusion drawn from this study, therefore, was that humans will use as much time as they are given to complete a task, regardless of how simple or complex the task might be. And, furthermore, dramatically shrinking the amount of time one spends on a given task will not necessarily result in a lower level of quality.

I can relate to this study because, many years ago, I found myself working at a job where I seemed to be spending all day answering emails. It was frustrating. I was routinely spending somewhere between five and six hours every single day simply dealing with problems and questions, and replying to emails. I was desperate to reduce the amount of time I spent on email each day. I tried a number of different tricks, but nothing seemed to work. But then, for some reason, I got an idea, and I decided to try an experiment. I decided that I would dedicate one hour in the morning to answering emails, and then another half hour before the end of my day. This meant that, instead of spending six hours of my day in my inbox, I would spend no more than one and a half hours per day reading and writing emails.

I remember the first day I tried it. I was amazed by how fast I whipped through emails. I knew I didn't have much time, so I was firing them off faster than I thought possible. At the end of the day I had responded to all the emails in my inbox in one quarter of the time it usually took me! I couldn't believe it. I assumed this day must have been different. Maybe I had a lot of easy emails that day. Or maybe the volume was lower than usual. But, the same thing happened the next day and the next day and the next. My week was completely revolutionized simply by changing the amount of time I gave myself to answer emails.

But it didn't take long until I realized something else. I had reduced the amount of time I was spending on email, but my day was still flying by. It turns out there were a thousand other small tasks that had rushed in to claim my time. I now had extra time each day, but I wasn't getting more done. Instead, I was using this extra time on a bunch of other small, unimportant tasks. I had just allowed other tasks to expand and take up my new-found time.

I knew I needed to make another change. I decided to keep a pad beside me on my desk, and any time a small task came up that threatened to take my time, I jotted it down. Then, near the end of the day, I would spend thirty minutes frantically getting all the little things done that I had written down. These tasks that previously had occupied my entire day could be done in thirty minutes, as long as I knew I had a deadline. I didn't realize it at the time, but I was beginning to harness the power of the Law of Expansion.

As I continued to give myself strict time-limits for each of my tasks, I found that I was getting more things done and that I was able to spend much more time focused on bigger projects and pursuing new opportunities. While my colleagues were still swamped with email and the other small, time-consuming tasks we all had to do each day, I was getting my email out of the way and all my small tasks done in less than two hours. This meant I could spend the rest of my day focused on big projects that would really move the needle and make a difference in my career. It was great.

I wish that I could say that everything was smooth sailing after that, but it wasn't. You see, the Law of Expansion is always at work. This means that, even today, I have to be careful to guard my time. I have found that if I don't set strict time-limits for myself, my productivity will drop by at least 50% on the first day, and it will keep going down each subsequent day that I let it.

Abiding by the Law of Expansion means that you have to constantly guard your time. It takes a lot of work to keep each little task at bay because it pushes relentlessly to take as much time as possible. Your tasks will conspire against you, if you allow them. They will expand to fill up as much time as they can so they can keep you unproductive. But, once you know about the Law of Expansion and begin to use it to your advantage, you will become the most productive person in the office by a mile.

27. The Law of the Lion and the Frog

If it's your job to eat a frog, it's best to do it first thing in the morning. And if it's your job to eat two frogs, it's best to eat the biggest one first.

—Mark Twain

The Law of the Lion and the Frog states that success requires a commitment to do difficult things. We all have certain things in our lives that we find difficult. These are the things we usually put off, if possible. But, more often than not, these are also the things that will bring us closer to our goals.

For a lot of people, working out is something they dread. We all know we need to take care of our bodies, but going to the gym is one of those things that is really easy to put off until "later." And so many people do. Other people put off managing their household budget. Everyone knows that spending more money than you make is a recipe for disaster, but a lot of people don't ever track where their money is going because they hate the thought of living with a budget. Maybe for you it's a meeting you need to have with your boss. Maybe it's doing the laundry. Or maybe it's cold-calling clients. It doesn't matter what it is, we all have something (or, more likely, multiple things) in our lives that we don't want to do, even though we know it's important.

To have success, you must develop the ability to do difficult things, even when you don't feel like it. Mark Twain is famously quoted as saying, "If it's your job to eat a frog, it's best to do it first thing in the morning. And if it's your job to eat two frogs, it's best to eat the biggest one first." His point is that, if eating a frog is on your to-do list for tomorrow, it's probably the worst thing you will have to do all day. It's the one thing you will be dreading. And it's the one thing you will be tempted to put off until "later." But, if you get up and do it immediately, you can at least go through the rest of your day knowing that you've finished your most dreaded task for the day. You will be happy and motivated to take on the rest of your day, knowing that the worst is behind you. But, if you don't tackle that task first, if you put off eating the frog until later, you will go through the rest of your day dreading what you know is still coming. You won't be focused or motivated to do anything all day because the fact that you have to eat a frog later is hanging over your head, whether you consciously recognize it or not.

The human brain is not wired for discomfort. In fact, it is wired to avoid discomfort. Just think, what do most of us try and do when we're in an uncomfortable situation? We leave. We run away. That's how we're wired. Anytime we start to feel just a little discomfort, our immediate reaction is to try and get out of the situation. If there's even a small chance we could avoid eating the frog altogether, we'll take it. We'll put off doing it until later because we know that we might be able to put off doing it again. And if we keep putting it off long enough, we can avoid doing it altogether.

The problem, of course, is that the thing we want to run away from—that thing that causes us discomfort—is very often the most important thing we should be doing. Every time you put off exercise, you increase your chance of having health complications later in life. Every time you put off balancing your budget, you reduce your chances of attaining financial freedom. The things we put off have consequences, regardless of whether we see those consequences today or not.

To have success, you need to develop the ability to do the things you don't want to do. You need to be able to eat your frogs every single day. It needs to be a pattern of behavior. It needs to be part of your mindset.

You need to adopt the mindset of a lion. Imagine if a lion had to eat a frog for breakfast. What do you think he would do? Would he put it off because it made him uncomfortable? Of course not. A lion would attack that frog without thinking twice about it. That frog wouldn't stand a chance. One bite and it would be over. That's because a lion is wired to attack. A lion doesn't have to think about whether it should attack its prey. It just does it. It's built into its DNA.

You, too, can develop your ability to attack your frogs, whatever they might be. You can become like a lion, where attacking your frogs is instinctive. But it will take time. At first, it will be a struggle. But after a while, the positive results of attacking your most dreaded task every day will start to pay off. You will start to see progress in that area. You will start to see actual results. Attacking your most dreaded task every day will put you in a different mindset. Eventually you will learn to look forward to eating that frog because you know what it will do for your day and, eventually, for your life.

But until that point, you will need to take steps to build momentum. The best way to do this is to simply think about everything preventing you from eating your frog and then remove those things one by one. I know people who go so far as sleeping in their gym clothes just to remove the barrier of having to get dressed for the gym in the morning. When you wake up in your gym clothes, your brain has to decide to consciously take off those clothes and put on other clothes for work. It reverses the barrier facing the brain. Instead of protesting that it's too much of a hassle to put on clothes for the gym, the brain now sees taking off the gym clothes as the bigger obstacle. As a result, leaving the gym clothes on and actually going to the gym becomes the easier decision. Your brain doesn't want to consciously prevent you from going to the gym; it just wants to put it off. So if you wake up ready to go, it makes it just that much easier to push through and get your workout done.

Whatever your frog is, think about the barriers that are holding you back. Think about the excuses you tell yourself, and think about the reasons why you're putting it off. Then, as you remove these excuses one by one, you will find that you are able to start doing that thing instead of putting it off. And, once you've begun to build momentum, you will start to develop a lion mindset. You will find that you can start getting up ready to attack your frog without thinking twice. If you do this, you will start to see success.

28. The Law of the Core

If disproportionate results come from one activity, then
you must give that one activity disproportionate time.
—Gary W. Keller

T he Law of the Core states that there are always a small
set of actions and skills that are most important for
success. Most of our lives are jammed with all kinds
of tasks and responsibilities. But, in reality, only a small
subset of the things we do each day are responsible for the
majority of our results.

There's a well-known principle, called the Pareto
Principle, which states that 20% of all causes produce 80%
of all outcomes. This principle was first discovered by the
Italian civil engineer and economist, Vilfredo Pareto, in
1896. One day, while he was harvesting peas in his garden,
Pareto noticed that most of the peas he was harvesting
appeared to come from a relatively small number of pods.
This was surprising, since one would reasonably expect that
each peapod would have roughly the same number of peas
in it. But, after taking the time to count them, Pareto found a
very different result. He found that 80% of the peas he
harvested in his garden came from 20% of the pods. So, of

the twenty pods he initially selected to examine, he found that eighty peas came from just four of the pods. This means that four pods produced more peas than the other sixteen pods combined. And this ratio held true for the entire garden.

As an economist, Pareto began to explore whether this same pattern was at work more generally in the world. To his surprise, he found that about 20% of the people who lived in Italy at the time made 80% of the money and owned 80% of the land in the country. Thus was born the Pareto Principle.

Since Pareto's initial observation, the Pareto Principle has been found to be operative in pretty well every single sphere of life. Generally, 20% of criminals produce 80% of all crimes. Business owners typically find that 20% of their customers account for 80% of sales. In a workplace, 20% of the people will generally do 80% of the work. Non-profits report that 80% of their donations come from 20% of their donors. This principle is everywhere.

You can apply this principle to your own life as well. You will accomplish 80% of your work in 20% of your time. You will find that 20% of your tasks produce 80% of your results. You can read 20% of a book and get 80% of the benefit. And so on.

The most successful people use this principle to their advantage. Let me tell you about my friend Jake. Jake is a salesman, and he makes is money only by commission. When I met Jake a few years ago, he was an average salesman in his company. He was making right around ten sales per week, which meant that he was making about $70,000 per year. This was almost exactly what the average sales rate was for the company where he worked. But Jake wanted more. He wanted to become the best salesman in his company.

When Jake and I first began working together, we spent some time figuring out what his core actions were. We wanted to identify the 20% of his week that was producing 80% of his results. After a little trial and error, we were able to identify a set of actions that were responsible for roughly 80% of his success. In his case, the core 20% included following up with existing clients and working on landing large new accounts. We found that, while he was spending nearly 80% of his time trying to land smaller accounts, these efforts were only contributing roughly 20% to his bottom line.

After identifying his core actions, Jake's path to success was clear: he needed to double down on them. This meant, instead of spending 20% of his time following up on existing clients and landing larger new ones, he focused on consistently spending 40% of his time on these actions over twelve months. At first it was tough. He had already developed habits and patterns that were tough to break. But, after a few months, new habits and patterns began to take over. And at the end of the year, Jake increased his income from $70,000 to $110,000.

But here's where things get really interesting. Jake was motivated to double down even further. He was happy with the progress he had made, but he wanted more. So we went through the same process again, this time based on his new patterns and behaviors. Once again, we looked at his core actions and identified the 20% of those actions that were producing 80% of the results. We found that he was getting the vast majority of his results from 20% of his time working with large clients in two very specific industries. So, we zeroed in on those industries further. And, again, we worked together for the next few months. Jake, once again, doubled the amount of time he spent working with clients in those specific industries. At the end of the year he called me to report that he had earned $180,000 that year and was named salesperson of the year in his company.

But here's the really crazy part. Because things were going so well for Jake that year, he almost completely eliminated having to drum up smaller clients. In other words, by following the Law of the Core, Jake completely eliminated the things he used to spend 80% of his time on when we first met. This meant that, in the end, not only did Jake more than double his salary, he also cut down on the hours he spent working. He got more done in less time because he focused on his core actions.

The Law of the Core is incredible because you can break things down over and over again. So, while it is true that you should focus on your most important 20%, it is also true that 20% of your 20% will produce 80% of your 80%. In other words, 4% of your actions will produce 64% of your results. Just imagine: what if you could identify the 4% of your actions that are most important. And what if you could add skills and competencies that could multiply the effectiveness of that 4%? You could effectively reduce your workweek to one-and-a-half hours and get the exact same results you currently get working forty hours.

Now, here's were it gets really crazy. You can do 20% of your 4% and get done 80% of your 64%. In other words, less than 1% of your actions are producing just over 50% of your results. Imagine if you could identify what that 1% is. You would be able to focus your attention on those tasks and you could even double down on them.

That's why identifying your core is so important. Not only will it help you focus on the things that are most important for your current results, but it will also tell you where you can improve in order to multiply those results.

And this is important because making improvements to your core will have disproportionate results. If you could identify the 1% of your actions that are producing 50% of your results each week, and then double your effectiveness in executing on those actions, you would create the same results you are currently getting with 1% of the effort.

All of this might sound crazy. But it's true. I've seen it happen time and time again. I've done it in my own life, and I've helped other people do it in theirs. Anybody can do it, if they just know how.

Practically speaking, the process is really quite simple. First, you have to identify your core. You need to figure out the 20% of your actions that are producing 80% of the results. The best way to do this is to track exactly what you do each day for a few weeks. Then, look at what you've achieved over that time and determine which actions from your list led to which results. You probably won't be able to link every action to particular results, but a core group of actions should begin to emerge as most important for you. At this point, you will have a sense of what your core actions are.

Next, you need to work to increase the time and effort you spend on these core actions. This will likely mean you need to find ways to decrease the time you're spending on everything else. Because you've already tracked your activity for a few weeks, you should have a good sense of how you're spending your time. So this step will be relatively straightforward. Simply return to the record you kept of your activities and see where you can trim some time off the activities that make up your 80%. The time is definitely there. You just need to find it.

Then, commit to spending double the time and effort each day on the core activities you identified in step one. Do this for thirty days, and your life will change. I promise you.

After you've done this, you can repeat the process over and over again. Each time you do, you will get a clearer sense of what your core activities are and the skills you need to execute on them. Then, once you've isolated the most important skills, you can work to improve them. When you get to this point in the process, success is inevitable.

29. The Law of the Keys

In the midst of an ordinary day, I try to remind myself that I am preparing for the extraordinary.
— Shalane Flanagan

The Law of the Keys states that there are certain activities that are valuable because they unlock the ability to perform your core activities at the highest level. Very often, these actions are what we would consider "ordinary" and, therefore, seem unimportant. But they aren't. They are essential for success.

Usually, your core activities which I spoke about in the previous chapter will require specific skills. You might need to be good at sales, singing, thinking, teaching, or any number of other things in order to have success at whatever you're pursuing. The importance of these skills is usually fairly obvious. If you want to be a writer, for example, you need to develop skills that will make you a better writer. That's obvious.

But, what is much less obvious are the actions you need to take in order to ensure that you are able to perform your core activities at the highest level possible. These are what I call key activities because they are like the keys that unlock your ability to perform your core activities.

For example, one of the core activities in my life is spending time reading, singing, and talking with my kids before they go to bed. Every night, my kids know that they get at least an hour of my undivided attention. They look forward to it, and so do I. Of course, I enjoy spending as much time with my kids as possible, but the time we spend together each night before they go to bed has a disproportionate result on their development and our relationship. It's sacred. That's why it's part of my core 20%.

But, in order to maximize the impact of this precious time I spend with my kids each night, I need to consistently perform a number of key activities as well. For example, during this time, we read a lot of books together. I love books, and I want my kids to grow up loving books, too. One of the ways I try to foster their excitement for books is by adding new books to our home library on a regular basis. When the kids know that they have a new book to read, they get excited, and I love that. So, this means that one of my key activities is to order new books for them every week. It doesn't take long, but it's something I have to do in order to make our time together as meaningful as possible.

Similarly, I have found that I am at my best each and every day when I go to bed at 10 p.m., get up at 5 a.m., and exercise for at least thirty minutes at some point during the day. Of course, eating well is important, as is spending time with family and friends. But, for me, if I take care of going to bed at the right time, getting up at the right time, and fitting in thirty minutes of exercise every day, the other pieces of my day seem to fall into place much easier. So I consider going to bed, getting up, and exercise as my key activities each day. In and of themselves, they aren't going to bring me a lot of success because they don't belong to my core activities. But, they make it possible for me to achieve success.

If you don't pay appropriate attention to the key activities in your life, your core will suffer. The most successful people create lives where everything they do is either a core activity or a key activity. They are either focused on their most important activities for success, or they are focused on activities that will enable them to excel at those core activities. This is why so many people talk about morning routines. Most people who achieve long-term success have some kind of morning routine. They might get up early to meditate, journal, or pray. They might exercise, drink coffee, or read the paper. There's no exact formula that works for everyone. But the people who make the most of their day usually take the time to make sure they do the things in the morning that will unlock success for them later in the day.

The Law of the Keys also applies to skills. Just as there are key activities that help you to perform your core activities, so also there are certain skills that help you excel at your core activities. These are your key skills. For example, if you are a writer, one of the skills you will likely need to perform the core activity of writing is the skill of typing on a keyboard. The more efficient you are at typing, the faster you will be able to write. Therefore, one of the key skills that could help you become more effective as a writer would be being able to type fast. This is not a necessary skill you must possess in order to have success as a writer. But, being able to type more efficiently will allow you to write faster. Because of this, becoming efficient at typing on a keyboard could very well be a key skill that helps you perform one of your core activities.

In a similar way, being able to navigate the word processing program you use is also an important skill to have as a writer. Not only will it save you time, but knowing about various features might allow you to include new features into your writing from time to time that would improve your writing overall. That's a good thing. So, once again, being well-versed in your word processor is not an essential skill to find success as a writer, but it is an important skill that unlocks the possibility of writing well.

Again, having a better understanding of sentence structure would help to make your writing engaging, which will, almost certainly, help you find success as a writer. It is not the sole skill that will determine whether or not you find success as a writer, but because it helps to make good writing possible, it would likely serve as one of your key skills.

In the case of each of these skills—the ability to type efficiently, navigating your word processor, and understanding sentence structure—they alone do not constitute the core activity of writing. In fact, you can perform your core activity of writing with only the bare minimum level of proficiency in each of these areas. But each of these skills could have a direct impact on your core activity. Therefore, they are key skills.

The reason this law is so powerful is that it draws attention to the importance of what you do in domains that might appear to be outside of your core. Every time you assume that what you do when you're not working on your core activities doesn't impact them, you are ignoring this law. On the other hand, once you recognize that you can engage in activities and develop skills that unlock the possibility of achieving new levels of success in your core activities, you can begin to achieve success by design.

30. The Law of Significance

What is important is seldom urgent and what is urgent
is seldom important.

—Dwight Eisenhower

The Law of Significance states that urgency does not
determine importance. Put another way, you could
say that the things you should be doing at any
moment are almost never the things you feel pressure to do,
and the things you feel pressure to do are almost never the
things you should be doing. Think about it for a minute.
What urgent tasks have you faced this week? What things
did you *have* to do? Did you *have* to print off a document
your boss urgently needed? Did your friend *need* to talk on
the phone? Did you receive an email from a client that *had*
to have an immediate response? We are all faced with
hundreds of urgent tasks like these every single day. They
are tasks that *need* to be done, and they *can't* be put off.

But the problem with urgent tasks is that they almost
certainly will not help you accomplish your goals in life.
Printing off a document for your boss probably isn't going
to get you a promotion. Calling your friend back isn't going
to get you a publishing deal. Responding to all your emails

within twelve hours isn't going to help you double your income.

Here's a good rule of thumb: *when you feel pressure to do something, that's a sign that it likely serves someone else's goal, not yours.* Why do you feel like you *have* to respond to emails as fast as you can? You might think it's because you want to be seen as an efficient colleague or partner, but it's far more likely that you've fallen victim to the trap of allowing other people to set your agenda. Just think about it. If one of your goals for the day is to empty your inbox before you leave the office, you've effectively decided that helping other people reach their goals is more important than reaching your own.

Don't get me wrong. There are many urgent tasks that are worth doing. And helping other people reach their goals can be a very rewarding thing. But, it is important that you understand that, when it comes to success in your own life, spending your time on "urgent" tasks will not get you where you want to go. You don't have to like it, but it's the way things are. It's a law. Most people I've met try to work against the Law of Significance because they constantly allow all their "urgent" tasks to take precedence over everything else. But, if you let them, those tasks will end up filling up your life.

You might be thinking that you're unique. Your urgent tasks actually are urgent, right? Well, let me tell you a story about two friends of mine, Allison and Bryce. A few years ago, Allison and Bryce had a lot going on. They were entrepreneurs who were trying to build a new business; they had just had a new baby; and they had recently bought a new house. One day, while I was talking to them, they confided in me that, while they were very excited to be new parents and homeowners, they were having a difficult time making

177

progress in their business with everything else going on. The baby was demanding all their time and energy. On top of that, there was a never-ending list of things to do on their new house. They told me that they didn't have enough time or energy left to spend on the things they knew they needed to do in order to make their business successful. Every time they sat down to work, they were either too tired to make much progress or there was something else that urgently needed to be done. The bell on the washing machine would ring, reminding them that the laundry needed to be transferred to the dryer. One of their parents would stop by to see the baby, and they would be reminded that the house needed decorating and baby-proofing. Whenever it rained, it would remind them that they needed to build a new shed to store their tools. All the empty space in their new house would constantly tell them that they needed to go furniture shopping. It seemed like they continually needed to run to the store to buy groceries, diapers, and pacifiers. On top of all this, their dog needed to be walked, the lawn needed to be mowed, and family and friends coming over to visit the baby needed to be entertained. Allison and Bryce had a whole slew of urgent tasks that seemed, well, *urgent*. The problem was that all of these urgent tasks meant that work on their business kept getting put off until later. But later wasn't coming around.

Eventually, it got to the point where things were getting desperate. Bryce told me one day that he was beginning to doubt whether they could even make a go of their business anymore. He asked me for advice. So I told him plainly that, from what I could tell, they were violating the Law of Significance. The solution, I said, is to begin by prioritizing the significant over the urgent. I explained that, while they might feel like they need to buy new furniture or build a shed this week, having a new couch or a new place to store their tools won't bring them any closer to their long-term goals. Sure, these things would be nice. But they aren't significant enough to make them a priority. Right now, I told him, the most direct route to their long-term goals was to continue to build a successful business. If they landed a couple new clients in their business this week, they might just be able to devote a morning to go furniture shopping next week.

Bryce and Allison took my advice. They started to prioritize their business ahead of anything around the house. Yes, there were still urgent tasks that needed to get done. The dog still needed to get walked, and the baby still needed to be cared for. But they stopped worrying about cutting their grass every week or about being the perfect hosts when guests popped by to see the baby. And, little by little, they started to notice significant progress in their business. It took them a few months until business was booming again, but it eventually happened.

It's funny how things work out. Once their business was back on track, Allison and Bryce seemed to have more time and energy. As long as they were prioritizing their significant tasks, it seemed that they had enough time to get all their urgent tasks done as well. This is because it's a lot easier to fit a few half hour tasks into a full schedule than it is to fit an entire work day into a schedule stacked full of half hour tasks. I remember speaking with Bryce a few months after our initial conversation, and he expressed his amazement by this. He simply couldn't believe that this worked exactly how I predicted.

That's the Law of Significance.

31. The Law of Growth

Everything will change. The only question is growing up or decaying.

—Nikki Giovanni

The Law of Growth states that success requires ongoing improvement. This is because nothing in the world ever remains static. Everything is always changing. Things are decaying, dying, and being replaced every single day. The atoms and cells that make up the human body are completely replaced every seven years. Your car will rust and your clothes will fade. Both will be replaced. Your relationships will either grow and mature, or they will shrink and die, just like plants. They either grow, or they die. In our world, there is decay, or there is growth. But there is nothing that stays exactly the same.

The same is true of success. Either you are moving toward it or you are moving away from it. You cannot ever be standing still. If you are not improving, you are falling behind. If you are not growing, you are shrinking. So, if you want to achieve success, you need to be growing and improving every day.

Now, recognizing the Law of Growth at work in every area of life, it is possible to use this law to your advantage by focusing on strategic improvement. Recall the Law of the Core I discussed earlier. According to that law, there are a core set of activities and skills that are responsible for the majority of your success. If you've figured out which of your skills belong to your core, learning to improve your core skills is the fastest and surest way to harness the power of this law.

I heard somewhere that we should all try to be 1% better every day. I don't know who originally came up with this idea, but I have found it to be helpful. It's a good marker to shoot for because, while 1% might not seem like very much, it is enough to all but guarantee your success. Just think, if you improve on the skills you need to succeed by just 1% each day, you will improve by more than 3,600% in one year. Imagine being thirty-six times better at your most important skills one year from now. What would that do for your success? If you were to put a monetary value on your improvement, it would be like going from earning a salary of $50,000 to earning $1,800,000 in the course of a single year.

The reason this is possible is because there is a compound effect at work. If you improve by 1% today, that means tomorrow's 1% is bigger than today's 1%. And the next day's 1% is bigger still. And so on. Just to give you a sense of how this works, in seventy days, you would double your proficiency in whatever skill you are working to improve upon. In one hundred and ten days, or about four months, you would triple your proficiency. In one hundred and forty days, or five months, you would quadruple your proficiency. In about one hundred and sixty days, you would improve your proficiency by 500%.

But things get really crazy when you choose to focus on the right things. You will recall that, according to the Law of the Core, 4% of your actions are yielding 64% of your results. If you were able to isolate the 4% of tasks that make up your core and focus your energy on improving 1% each day at the skills required for those actions, not only could you improve your core skills by 3,600% in a year, but these improvements would have incredible ripple effects on the rest of your life. Because that core 4% has a disproportionate influence on your results, improving your skills by 3,600% could potentially increase your results by more than 192,000%. Yes, you read that correctly. By improving by 1% at the *right skills* every single day, you will not only double or triple your results. You can increase your results by nearly 200,000%.

Now, I realize that most of us are not going to put in the time and effort required to make this kind of progress. But by harnessing the power of the Law of Growth even part of the time will yield incredible results. Imagine if you only achieve half of the results I cited above, or even a quarter of those results. That would still be incredible. The reason I rattle off these big numbers is to show you how, once you recognize that growth or decay are your only options, pursuing growth consistently over time can easily double, triple, or quadruple your results. If it's possible for someone to improve their output by more than 192,000% in a year, then surely it's possible for you to improve your output by ten-fold this year, right?

Just imagine what kind of impact that would have on your life. What kind of difference would a ten-fold increase make to your relationships? What kind of difference would it make to your lifestyle? What kind of difference would it make to your confidence? Really think about it for a minute:

how big of a deal would it be for you to improve your output by ten-fold in one area of your life? I'm betting it would be huge.

If so, what are you waiting for? Get down to figuring out your core and then commit to improving on that core by 1% every day. If you do this, you will be harnessing the power of the Law of Growth. And, once you do that, you won't be able to stop yourself from achieving success.

32. The Law of Evaluation

Edit your life frequently and ruthlessly. It's your masterpiece after all.

—Nathan W. Morris

The Law of Evaluation states that regular and proper evaluation is essential for success. I speak regularly with people who want to improve the results they see in their lives. But, when I ask them to talk about how they are currently measuring their results, they give me a blank stare. They have never thought about formally evaluating their lives. However, the reality is that success will very often be proportionate to the quality of the evaluations one conducts.

John Robert Wooden, NCAA basketball coach of the UCLA Bruins for twenty-seven years, won ten NCAA national championships with the Bruins, including seven in a row. When asked about the success he enjoyed, he said: "Without proper self-evaluation, failure is inevitable." In my own experience, I have found this to be true. But I have also found the opposite to be true more often than not: with proper self-evaluation, success becomes inevitable. That is why the Law of Evaluation is one of the most important laws you should follow—if you're serious about having success, that is.

Evaluation is a method for ascertaining value. We commonly use the word "evaluation" as a general term any time we make a judgement. We tell people that they need to re-evaluate their priorities, or we say that we are evaluating whether or not we should make a big purchase. While we all use the term in this way from time to time, technically speaking, it is incorrect. There is an entire academic sub-field devoted to the study of evaluation, and scholars in this field work with a much more technical definition of the term than most of us are used to. The simplest form of this definition is the one provided by the American Evaluation Association. They define evaluation like this: "Evaluation is the systematic process to determine merit, worth, value, or significance." Notice that evaluation, here, is not a general assessment made from a list of pros and cons; it is *systematic*. That is to say, it is a repeatable, intentional process that has clearly defined steps. Furthermore, this process is focused squarely on determining the ultimate value of whatever is being evaluated. To conduct an evaluation, then, means doing more than simply thinking in general terms about how things are going. It means having clearly defined metrics and using a repeatable process to measure progress being made toward specific goals. Conducting an evaluation is, in this sense, scientific.

The reason I am beginning my discussion of this law by talking about the technical definition of evaluation is because the process of evaluation is almost always poorly executed. And that is because it is rarely understood in its proper, technical sense. Either it is not systematic enough, or it is not clearly focused on determining value in any measurable way. This is true at the individual level and at the corporate level. Too often, evaluations end up looking a lot more like reflections. It is good to reflect, to think back over a period of time. But that's not the same thing as evaluation.

There are a lot of components that go into a good evaluation. But, when it comes to evaluating your personal progress toward a specific goal, the number one principle to keep in mind is the principle of return on investment (ROI). When it comes to ROI, the question is always the same: what are you getting out of what you're putting in? Every single thing you do has a return. Your job when conducting an evaluation is determining what effort, time, energy, or money you've invested in trying to reach a specific goal, and what that investment has yielded. Depending on your goal, this might mean that you have to track the amount of time you're spending on certain tasks every day, or you might have to record the amount of money you are using to buy materials on a separate ledger. Only you can determine exactly what steps you need to take to give yourself the data you need in order to conduct your assessment. When you've determined what you've gained and what you've invested, you will have your ROI.

Once you have your ROI, you will need to take things one step further. Remember, the whole goal of conducting an evaluation is to determine the value of your actions. In order to do this, you will need to map your ROI onto your larger plan. So, for example, if your goal is to lose thirty pounds in a year, it would be reasonable for you to expect to have lost about fifteen pounds in the first six months. But if you find that you've only lost five pounds at the six-month mark, your evaluation will show you exactly what you've invested (time in the gym and diet) in order to lose five pounds.

With that data in hand, you can adjust your course for the rest of the year. Either you will lower your weight loss expectations for the year from thirty pounds to 10 pounds, or you will have to increase your investment. In the case of some goals, doing an evaluation might help you realize that the return is not worth the investment required. That's okay.

The great thing about conducting evaluations is that they allow you to literally predict success because they provide you with your rate of return. When you conduct proper evaluations, you find out exactly what you've invested and what your return is on that investment. And so you know exactly what you have to invest going forward to get the return you want. Evaluations give you the formula for success. As a result, success becomes simple. The Law of Evaluation is so powerful because following it enables you to easily calculate your success.

However, when you don't conduct evaluations, or you don't conduct them properly, you violate the Law of Evaluation. As a result, success remains a mystery to you. At best, it's a guessing game. When you violate the Law of Evaluation, you give up all your predictive power.

Depending on the goal(s) you're working toward, you should be conducting evaluations on the weekly, monthly, quarterly, and yearly marks. Doing this will allow you to make adjustments as needed. Building on the example I used above, conducting an evaluation at the six-month mark means that it would be highly unlikely for that person to hit their target of losing thirty pounds by the end of the year. Finding out that they've only lost five pounds in six months doesn't leave them much time to make up the difference. However, if they were conducting weekly and monthly evaluations, they would have been able to adjust their investment much sooner, making it possible to increase their results much sooner as well and so hit their goal.

When it comes to achieving success in life, the Law of Evaluation cannot be broken. If you do not evaluate, you will not succeed. Period. This is because you will not be able to predict which actions to take in order to get the results you want. Success, for you, will constantly be a guessing game. Sure, you might randomly achieve something once in a while. But you won't be able to maintain any significant level of success.

But if you consistently conduct thorough evaluations of your progress on a regular basis, you are much more likely to succeed. In fact, if you don't just learn the Law of Evaluation, but if you actually master it, you will be able to predict your own success.

33. The Law of the Student

Continuous learning is the minimum requirement for
success in any field.

—Brian Tracy

The Law of the Student states that success requires
becoming a good student. This is an irrefutable law.
It cannot be ignored or violated. It isn't optional. It
isn't a suggestion. If you aren't constantly learning,
whatever level of success you currently enjoy will soon
disappear.

In the first place, this law means that, if you want to have
success, you must constantly pursue opportunities to learn.
Regardless of whether you're pursuing formal education or
not, you need to be reading books and articles, listening to
lectures and podcasts, talking with people who know things
you don't know, and seeking out coaches and mentors.
These are all important ways to keep learning.

But the Law of the Student goes deeper than this. It's not
just about learning; it's also about something more
fundamental: it's about an attitude toward learning. The
word "student," in its original Latin form, means to be
"eager" or "zealous" for true knowledge. Taking this

definition seriously, we can see how it is possible to learn from books and mentors without ever becoming a student in the true sense of the word. To follow the Law of the Student, and to be able to use it to maximize your success, you need to cultivate a legitimate and sincere desire to learn, regardless of whatever preconceived notions you might have had.

There's an important difference between learning and being a student. I have spent a large portion of my life in the classroom, first as a student, and then as a teacher. In my experience, I have found that what separates those who simply learn from those who become true students is their attitude. Everyone in the class engages in the same basic behaviors: they listen, think, and speak. But, when true students listen, they pay attention to what is being said by the teacher and by their classmates. When they think, they take what they hear and read seriously, they try and understand it from the other person's perspective, and they try honestly to make sense of it. And, when they speak, they ask genuine questions and offer sincere opinions.

Those who are mere learners still listen, think, and speak. But everything they hear gets filtered through a lens that confirms whatever they thought previously. They think, but only about how others are wrong. When they speak, they spout platitudes and propaganda. Mere learners can still learn the same facts and concepts as the true student, but they aren't eager to pursue true knowledge. They care more about what the things they learn can do for them and their goals than about the value of learning itself.

The difference between merely learning and being a student comes down to the fact that those who merely learn try to control the process. They're only interested in what they learn if it can serve their purpose in some way. And, once they find something that serves their purpose, they often stop learning altogether—until they need more ammunition for their cause. True students, on the other hand, allow what they learn to guide them. They enjoy having their preconceived notions challenged. They look forward to finding out something they hadn't predicted. And they never stop learning.

True students realize that every moment is an opportunity to pursue true knowledge. Books and lectures are important parts of learning, but they aren't the whole picture. Every experience, every person you meet, every conversation you have is an opportunity to gain knowledge. Successful people treat the entire world as their university.

We all feel the tendency to become mere learners at some point in our lives. It is tempting to use knowledge to confirm that we're right and others are wrong. But the faster you can transition from a mere learner to a true student, the faster you will achieve success. You can find some success by being a mere learner. You can pick up some tricks and hacks to get through life. But, there will always be a ceiling to your success. If, on the other hand, you take the approach of a true student, there is no telling how much success you can have.

The irony is that, while the mere learner pursues knowledge as a means to accomplish some preconceived goal, it is the true student—the one who pursues knowledge for its own sake—that ultimately finds success. So, if you want unlimited success, then work on developing the attitude of a true student. Work on becoming zealous for true knowledge. Don't settle for bits and pieces that confirm what you already believe. Seek out opportunities to have your thinking challenged, and take those opportunities seriously.

If you do, you will be well-prepared to have success in virtually every aspect of your life.

34. The Law of Action

Action is the foundational key to all success.
— Pablo Picaso

The Law of Action states that success requires action. This law might sound overly simplistic. But, simple or not, it is one of the easiest laws to violate without even realizing it. You see, success doesn't care about how much analysis you performed or how often you visualized achieving your goal. Of course, being properly prepared for success is important, but preparation by itself is never going to get you where you want to go. Eventually, you will need to actually *do* something. And only what you *do* will have any bearing on the success you achieve.

Your success, in many ways, will depend on how quickly you can transition from having an idea, researching it, and preparing yourself to take concrete action toward your goal.

We all have the tendency to confuse thinking with action. We all want to feel like we're making progress toward our goals. And the easiest way to get that feeling is to simply think about what we want to do, or what we should do, or what we plan on doing tomorrow, instead of actually doing it. Our brains are not very good at telling the difference between thinking about something and doing it, so it releases the same chemical reward in both instances. That's why it's so tempting to think about what you want to achieve instead of taking action. But, as Bruce Lee famously said, "If you spend too much time thinking about a thing, you'll never get it done." If you want to follow the Law of Action, you need to guard against this tendency in your life every single day.

One of the reasons why so many people find it difficult to fight this tendency is because they have developed the pattern of giving in to it. And once we develop patterns of behavior, they can be very difficult to break. Every time you spend more time than necessary thinking about something before you take action on it, you make it more likely that you'll do the same thing again next time.

One of the ways you can break this pattern is to make a conscious effort to shrink the amount of time between thinking and acting, even in little things. The more you can eliminate the time between thinking and action, the better it will be for you. So, next time you're watching a show and you think about having to take out the trash, force yourself to get up and do it right then. When you're relaxing and you think about sending a thank-you note to a friend, don't think about the exact words you plan on using; just get up and do it. Of course, you don't want to do these things if they are distracting you from something more important. If you're working on an important project or in a meeting, you probably shouldn't drop what you're doing to take out the trash. In that case, have a pad of paper with you and write the tasks down. Then, as soon as you are finished whatever it is you're doing, immediately take care of the small task before you move on to anything else.

If you do this, you will find over time that you get in the habit of taking action. Instead of sitting around thinking about what you want to do, or spending weeks "researching" your next step, your brain will start to prompt you to get into action mode. You will find that you start to look for action steps you can take. And once you get to that point, brace yourself because you will start to accomplish things you might not have thought possible.

However, here you have to be careful because this is when another tendency we all need to guard against usually pops up. As soon as you start to get your brain oriented to action, you will find that you will be tempted to do things that might not actually help you make progress. This is because your brain will not naturally distinguish between taking action and taking the *right* action. Once your brain is focused on action, it will naturally look for the simplest action you can perform, regardless of whether that action helps you make real progress. Always remember: just because your doing *something* doesn't mean you're making progress. Or, in the words of Ernst Hemmingway, "Never mistake motion for action."

Of course, making sure that you're doing the things that actually bring you closer to your goals requires thinking. The point of this law is not that you should eliminate thinking altogether. There always needs to be a process of assessment, and you should always make a plan before you act. But the key to using this law to your advantage is that you need to be able to shrink this process into a short time-span. The term "short" here is a relative term. For more complex or high-risk actions, your assessment and planning processes will likely take longer than it will for simpler actions. But the basic process is the same: focus on preparing yourself to take action as quickly as possible. In the end, I have found it helpful to keep these words from Gandhi in mind: "You may never know what results come from your action. But if you do nothing, there will be no result."

35. The Law of Mutual Benefit

> True greatness will be achieved through the abundant
> mind that works selflessly—with mutual respect, for
> mutual benefit.
>
> —Stephen Covey

The Law of Mutual Benefit states that success requires relationships where both parties help each other reach their goals. No matter who you are, you need to be able to work with other people, and you need to find people who are able to work with you, in order to have success. Even the most reclusive writer still needs to be able to work with her editor in some capacity, and the most awkward academic needs to be able to talk about his ideas with colleagues in order to have success. And the more you are able to help the people you work with have success, the more success you will have as well.

There is a story about Jim Rutherford, the long-time National Hockey League general manager, that helps illustrate this law well. Rutherford was one of the most successful general managers of his era. Not only did he enjoy a long career, but he was the manager of three Stanley Cup winning teams. He clearly knew a thing or two about success. One of the things he was well-known for was his willingness and ability to make trades with other teams. Some general managers struggled to make trades, but not Rutherford. He wasn't afraid to trade away good players for other good players, if he thought it would help his team win. Every year, it seemed like Rutherford was making a number of high-profile trades.

Near the end of his career as a manager, he was asked about his trading philosophy, and how he evaluated past trades he had made. Anytime there is a trade in sports, the media becomes obsessed with who "won" the trade. They spend hours analyzing every detail of the trade in an effort to determine which manager bested the other one. When Rutherford was asked about how he evaluated his own trades, most people were expecting him to talk about how he made trades to make his team better in the long-term, or how trades are really complex behind the scenes. These are the answers most general managers give. But what Rutherford said surprised everybody in the room. He said that he considered a trade to be successful if he could help his team *and also* help the other team he was trading with. In other words, part of his success included making his competition better. The media was clearly puzzled by this answer, so someone followed up asking for more clarity. Rutherford explained that, in order to have success over a long period of time in the NHL, a general manager needs to be able to work well with other general managers. Because other general managers saw that Rutherford was always fair, they were willing to do business with him time and time again. Because he was trying to help the teams he traded with, the other managers in the league *wanted* to work with him.

It might seem counter-intuitive, but Rutherford's commitment to helping other general managers find success was one of the keys to his own success. By making sure he was making trades that benefited his trading partners, everyone wanted to do business with him. The other managers who tried to "win" every trade soon found that they ran out of trading partners, but Rutherford always had a line of managers waiting to take his call. And, because everyone wanted to work with him, he was often able to pick and choose which trades would be the most beneficial for his team. Rutherford had success because he harnessed the power of the Law of Mutual Benefit.

Most of us probably aren't managing professional sports teams, but we all work with other people. And the way you treat those people might just be impacting your success more than you think. For example, almost every executive recruiter I have spoken to tells me that one of the most common mistakes job candidates make when going to a job interview is treating the administrative staff dismissively. Some people walk into the office thinking that they are somehow above the administrative assistants, and their body language shows it. But that's a big mistake because it violates the Law of Mutual Benefit. In many cases, the administrative assistant will be the person you actually work most closely with, and very often they are consulted before the management team makes a hire. To have success you will need to be sure to make their life as easy as possible. When you help them, it helps you.

When you truly harness the power of this law, you don't just make everyone's life easier. And you don't just make other people want to work with you. You will find that, if you follow the Law of Mutual Benefit—that is, if you genuinely try to work for the benefit of those around you— you will naturally build relationships with a wide range of different people, many of whom will have skills and expertise in areas that compliment your strengths. In the case of Jim Rutherford, not only did other managers want to work *with* him, but assistant managers and coaches wanted to work *for* him as well. In other words, he was often able to choose to bring people onto his management team that would add skills which he did not possess. As a result, achieving his goal of winning the Stanley Cup became a lot easier. In the same way, as you work to make sure those around you benefit from working with you, you are developing resources you can call on in future situations. This will allow you to marshal the skills and abilities other people possess to achieve success.

So, think about it for a minute: are you working toward mutual benefit in every interaction you have, or are you trying to get more out of other people than you give? Take a few minutes to honestly assess how well you are currently working with others for mutual benefit. And, if there are areas where you recognize you could align yourself more fully with this law, I encourage you to make the effort required to do so. If you follow this law, you will be reaping the benefits for years to come.

36. The Law of Communication

Communication—the human connection—is the key to personal and career success.

—Paul J. Meyer.

The Law of Communication states that one's chance of success rises and falls along with one's ability to communicate. Or, as the world-famous motivational speaker and businessman, Tony Robbins, has put it, "the quality of your life is the quality of your communication."

If you aren't having much success in a particular area of your life, very often it's because you are not communicating well. If those under your supervision aren't getting their work done, have a look at what you're communicating to them. If your marriage isn't as strong as you would like it to be, it's probably because your communication is off. If you're lacking motivation, consider what you are communicating to yourself. A lot of times, focusing on communication can go a long way to getting you where you want to go.

Now, when we think of communication, we most often think of things we actually say out loud. But that makes up only a very small fraction of human communication. In fact, most experts agree that somewhere between 70-90% of all communication is non-verbal. This means what we do, as well as how we do it, is usually much more important than what we say. There is a well-known rule in communication known as the 7-38-55 rule. This rule says that 7% of communication takes place through what we say, 38% of communication takes place through how we say it, and 55% takes place through body language and what we do.

Most of us are only mediocre communicators at best, but we might not even know it. I used to work as a consultant at a company where the manager I worked with had a reputation throughout the company as an excellent communicator. He would stand up in front of a crowd and have them spellbound for an hour. He was very good on stage. But, when I spoke with those who worked with him on a day-to-day basis, I found that a much different picture emerged.

Those who worked with him expressed frustration because he was actually a *bad* communicator. He would ask one of his employees to write up a report, only to not use it in the end. He would make a big deal about productivity tips and tricks around the office, but he would routinely take the afternoon off to go golfing. He would set targets for his team but then act like it didn't matter when they missed them.

The rest of the people in the office that he managed interpreted this as mixed messaging. He was saying one thing to them with his words, but then saying something else with his actions. It was frustrating for them. And his department ended up becoming extremely inefficient.

When I brought up the possibility that he was sending mixed messages to his team, this manager told me that he had never thought about it that way before. He had assumed that he had told them what he wanted and that was good enough. But, as George Bernard Shaw once remarked, "The biggest problem in communication is the illusion that it has taken place."

I explained to him that the employees didn't know that he was up every morning at 5 a.m. working from his home office, or that, when he rolled in late, it was because he was handling important calls from home before he came in. For all they knew, he might have been at the beach or watching cartoons all morning. Similarly, they didn't know that he hated golf, or that the only reason he went golfing was because it kept one of the company's most important clients happy. They assumed that he was blowing off work to spend time in the sun while they were all stuck in their cubicles. The employees didn't know that, when he asked one of them to write up a report, he wanted to compare their numbers with his own to make sure he was correct. He did this because he trusted their work more than his own. But they interpreted his actions to mean that he didn't value their work at all. They didn't know that, when he downplayed the seriousness of missing their targets, he was doing this because he didn't want them to feel bad about their performance. They assumed it meant he didn't care about the targets.

Upon hearing this, the manager was shocked. He had never thought about it that way. His immediate response was to try to explain all of this to his team. But I told him that, while that might be necessary, it wouldn't be enough. Even if the employees all knew that he was working all morning from home, for example, the fact that he rolls into the office late still communicates that managing his team isn't his top priority. The only solution is to be at the office every day before the rest of the team arrives. Only then will he clearly communicate his dedication to the team, and only then will he instill in everyone a strong sense that he is in control. In a similar way, he could tell them how much he values their work until he's blue in the face, but, unless he changes his actions, his team will still feel under-appreciated. When he asks them to run reports, he should actually *use* them, and he should give his team members credit.

The good news is that this manager did, in fact, make adjustments to his behavior. And, within a few weeks, his department's efficiency improved dramatically.

So, what are you communicating? Think about it long and hard. If you're always staying late after work, you're almost certainly communicating to your colleagues that you're behind. But if you're always there early, you will be communicating that you're ahead and that everything is under control. It doesn't matter whether you really *are* in control or not. The Law of Communication is entirely about what you are *communicating*.

Or again, if you're the kind of person who always takes the credit, you might think that you're letting people know how valuable you are, but, in reality, you're just telling them that you're annoying. Nobody wants to work with someone who takes all the credit. But if you constantly give credit away to others, even when you might deserve some yourself, you will be communicating to everyone that you're confident and generous.

Everything you do communicates something to those around you. If you have your phone in your hand every time you speak with your boyfriend, you're communicating something about how much you value him. But if you put down whatever you're working on every time he comes in the room, you will be telling him that he's important to you.

Or, if you don't have time to meet your father for lunch, you will be telling him that he's less important to you than all the mindless distractions you fill your day with. But, if he finds out that you moved a meeting just so you could see him, you will be communicating how much you value him.

Again, when you accept poor treatment without putting up a fight, you communicate that you are weak. And, on the flipside, if you're always standing up for yourself and your causes, you might very well be communicating that you're selfish. You might want to consider taking up a cause that doesn't benefit you once in a while, because this would communicate that you care about others' well-being as much as your own.

There are millions of other examples you could probably come up with from your own life. But the point is that everything you do communicates something. And, very often, we are completely oblivious to the things we are communicating most clearly to others.

The reality is that we can all become better communicators, no matter who we are. Nobody will master human communication. It is something you will have to constantly work on. But, as the composer John Powell once said, "Communication works for those who work at it." He's right. You don't have to become a great communicator tomorrow. Simply committing to work on your communication will naturally mean that you get better at it because it will make you conscious of what you're communicating. And this is the most essential step. So, if you're serious about success, you need to get serious about the Law of Communication.

37. The Law of the Brain

Your mind is for having ideas, not holding them.
                                                    —David Allen

The Law of the Brain states that the human brain has inbuilt limitations and biases that need to be overcome in order to achieve success. A lot of people sell themselves short because they think they aren't smart enough to achieve their dreams. But that's almost never true. Even the smartest people in the world need to use tools to help their brains accomplish most of what they do. Your brain, just like every human brain, is good at some things and not as good at other things.

The human brain is incredibly good at analyzing, thinking, deciphering and deciding. We can imagine things that don't exist. We can look into the past and dream about the future. At every single moment, our brains are taking in millions of pieces of information from our various environments, filtering that information, and presenting us with a usable pattern of the world. Despite all the advances of modern technology, the human brain is still the most complex and intelligent operating system on earth.

But the brain also has limitations. For instance, as David Allen has pointed out so clearly, the brain is not very good at holding onto ideas. Elizabeth Loftus, one of the foremost experts on the brain and memory, has shown that the brain constantly alters memories in ways that it thinks will make them more useful moving forward. Let's say, for example, two people witnessed a crime. They see what happened and then they talk about it. One person says they're pretty sure the perpetrator was wearing a yellow shirt. The other one thinks it was orange. Very often, one of the witnesses will change their memory to agree with the other one. They aren't trying to be deceptive. They actually believe that they are now remembering what really happened. The brain of that witness has determined that switching that minor detail of the memory is useful in some way.

There was a study conducted a number of years ago now trying to determine the reliability of what people remember about September 11, 2001. This, of course, was the tragic day when two airplanes were flown into the twin towers in New York City, in addition to another plane that crashed into the Pentagon and one that ended up crashing into a field. In this study, the research team interviewed more than three thousand people in New York, Washington, Boston, and four other cities across the USA. The team interviewed these participants one week after the attack, then again a full year after the attack, then again three years after the attack, and then, finally, ten years after the attack. The researchers found that most people remembered the main details of the attack accurately. But what was interesting was that their memories of virtually every other detail changed over time. They would typically misremember who they were with and change the way they described their feelings. Many of the participants closer to ground zero described their entire experience differently. For instance, as time passed, their recollection of what they heard, saw, and smelled changed. This study confirmed what researchers already knew about the brain's ability to store memories: it isn't very good at it.

The brain also does a very poor job of providing any kind of objectivity. We tend to go through the world thinking that the way we see and experience everything reflects the way things really are. And, while it *seems* to us that what we perceive is accurate, studies have shown that, very often, it isn't. Over the last few decades, researchers have found over and over again that the majority of people will report being above average when it comes to intelligence. Obviously, it's impossible for most people to be above average, so it is true that a large percentage of the population is mistaken about this. Similar studies have been conducted on people's self-perceptions around a variety of other things. For example, one study found that more than 90% of people report being better than the average driver. Another study found that most people predict that they will have more positive events occur in their lives than in other people's lives. In each of these cases, we can see that most people have perceptions about themselves and their experiences that are wrong.

This is due to something psychologists call "illusory superiority," which describes the tendency we each have to consider ourselves better than other people at most things.

Emily Pronin, a psychologist from Princeton University, has shown that most people are unable to recognize their own biases. She has shown that people who claim to be above average drivers actually believe that they are above average, regardless of how many car accidents they have been in. And people who believe that they possess above average intelligence will typically continue to believe this, no matter how many IQ tests they take. We all recognize that other people's opinions are biased, but we struggle to recognize that the very same biases are at work in us.

This is because, when people evaluate their own biases, they tend to focus on introspection. But when they evaluate the biases of others, they tend to rely on behavior. In other words, we effectively filter the way we interpret our own behavior by considering our good intentions and all of the various factors that might have influenced how we acted in a particular situation. If you had an argument with a friend and then got into a car accident, for example, chances are that this accident would not change whether you think you're a good driver or not. You would give yourself the benefit of the doubt because you recognize that there were mitigating circumstances. When it comes to other people, however, no such consideration is given. The fact that they get into a car accident makes you believe they aren't a good driver, regardless of what else might have been going on in their lives that day.

It is obvious how these conditions of the brain can be detrimental to success. If you are constantly thinking about your past and present in a way that is out of sync with reality, even just a little, the calculations you perform in order to make decisions about the steps you will take to pursue your goals will inevitably be out of whack. If you believe that you're an excellent driver, for example, you might incorrectly believe that your path to running a chauffeur service will be straightforward. Similarly, if you believe that you are more intelligent than average, you will likely underestimate the effort required for you to become a rocket scientist. These might be silly examples, but the point remains: if your brain is always remembering and evaluating things based on its own biases, rather than the objective facts, there are a myriad of ways you can get yourself into trouble. And people all over the globe have done just that.

However, by understanding a few general principles about how the brain works, we can actually turn these limitations into strengths. The brain, despite all its complexity, has a very clear purpose and function: it exists to help you move forward in the world. The reason why our brains even have memories is not so we can revisit them for nostalgic purposes, like you might look at a photo album or read entries from an old diary. No, the brain stores memories so that you can use them in the future. One of the reasons why we remember special events much more vividly than mundane events is because our brain has decided that there is something about those special events that might help us in the future. Remembering how much fun it was going for ice cream with your grandparents as a child is important because it serves as a signal for your brain to seek out similar experiences going forward. So, your brain remembers going for ice cream, even if it misremembers which ice cream you ate or what you were wearing. Similarly, the reason why we remember negative or traumatic experiences so well is because, once again, the brain sees them as important for future experiences: they mark out things to avoid.

Your brain is wired to keep you alive and to help you achieve your goals. Remembering things from the past that have no bearing on the future does not serve your brain's primary function. And so, it isn't good at it. Similarly, despite the fact that referees and umpires, judges and journalists, all profess to be objective, there is no such thing as an objective human brain. The human brain cannot be objective because it doesn't help you move through the world as well as allowing the inbuilt biases to persist.

The reason this is important is because it demonstrates what our brains are wired for and what they're not wired for. They're wired to help us move forward through life, but that means they aren't very good at looking at things the way they are. This isn't just true of memory, either. Our brains are easily biased by what we *want* to happen in the future. We've all had experiences where we convince ourselves that something will work out because we *want* it to, not because it has a legitimate shot at actually working out.

The fact that our brains are primarily concerned with preparing us for our future is an incredible strength. But, because of this, our brains sometimes alter facts in order to prepare us for the future that we want. This is a problem because, as we all know, just because you *want* something to work out doesn't mean it actually will work out.

Once we know about the brain's limitations, however, we can begin to use those limitations to help us achieve success. The simplest and most common way to do this is by making the brain's subjective analysis objective. In other words, success requires one to remove various details of one's journey from the brain and project them externally. This helps to remove the subjective biases inherent to the brain. Once the details are removed from the brain and spoken out loud or written down, the brain can look at those details not as its own but as something else. And, as we've already observed, our brains are much better able to look at things objectively when they're not about us.

By externalizing the data instead of leaving it internalized, you can effectively turn a major weakness into a strength. Being able to vocalize your thoughts to someone you trust is an excellent way to externalize your thoughts and, thereby, help your brain do its work. The great benefit of talking with another person is that it gives you the opportunity to receive feedback from a different brain—one that will be able to look at your thoughts more objectively. And that's priceless.

In addition, I always recommend that everyone pursuing success keep a journal of some kind. This is because writing has a strange ability to clarify thinking. The famous literary critic, William Zinsser, explained the importance of writing things down this way: "Writing organizes and clarifies our thoughts. Writing is how we think our way into a subject and make it our own. Writing enables us to find out what we know—and what we don't know—about whatever we're trying to learn." Zinsser's point here is that the process of writing helps your brain do its job of thinking. When you leave your thoughts in your head, you aren't aware of all the gaps in your thinking that your brain just skims over. But, as soon as you see your thoughts written out, those gaps become obvious.

By gaining greater clarity in your thinking through writing and speaking, you will also allow yourself to take the next step of analysis. This is so important. It requires second-order thinking. People who don't write to think often end up being a bit cloudy in what they think. They're unsure of what, exactly, they think, or why they think it. If they don't know what they think, they aren't able to analyze their thoughts. But, if you compare those people with people who write to think, you will see a world of difference. When you write your thoughts out, you gain clarity and have all your clearest thoughts externalized. You are able to look at it and examine them from multiple perspectives. That's so valuable that your analysis will be a hundred times better than if you don't write. And that could mean the difference between dramatically overachieving and severely underachieving.

38. The Law of the Chariot

Human behavior flows from three main sources: desire, emotion, and knowledge.

—Plato

The Law of the Chariot states that desire and emotion must be controlled in order to have success. We all have things we desire. Some of us desire power. Some of us desire money. Some of us desire relationships. Some of us desire meaning. Whatever you are pursuing in life, you can bet that you are pursuing it because you desire something. But the tricky thing is that we all desire multiple things at the same time, and very often our different desires pull us in opposite directions. The Law of the Chariot teaches us that we must find a way to control these desires, as well as the emotions they produce, by bringing them into alignment.

Plato was a famous philosopher. Despite the fact that he lived nearly 2,500 years ago, he is still considered by many to be the single most influential philosopher who ever walked the earth. In a book he wrote, called the *Phaedrus*, Plato talked about this very law. He said that each of us is like a chariot being pulled by two winged horses. In this analogy, the horses represent our desires and emotions. Desire is powerful. They are the reasons why we do anything instead of nothing. If we didn't desire food, we wouldn't eat. If we didn't desire love or relationships, we would have no friends. If we didn't desire entertainment, we would never watch movies. If you didn't desire success, you wouldn't be reading this book. If we didn't have desires, we would never pursue anything in life.

But Plato was a very wise man. He recognized that things are a bit more complicated than they might initially appear. He recognized that some of our desires are positive because they help us make progress toward our goals; but some of our desires are negative because they pull us away from our goals. Furthermore, he knew that these desires are often very closely related. For example, our desire for nourishment is positive because it motivates us to eat and, therefore, remain healthy. But our desire for consumption could easily hijack our positive desire for nourishment and cause us to overeat. In a similar way, our desire for love is positive because it drives us to form deep bonds with friends and family, which will greatly enhance the quality of our lives. But our desire for control can cause our relationships to become warped and dysfunctional quite easily if we're not careful. For every desire we have that motivates us to create positive results in our lives there will always be a desire that threatens to twist that positive desire and propel us in a direction that takes us away from our goals.

According to Plato, all the desires we have serve an important function in our lives. The trouble happens when we allow certain desires to take control and dominate some aspect of our lives. When that happens, our lives end up looking a lot like a chariot that isn't being properly controlled. The horses end up running wild, one pulling this way and the other pulling that way. The problem with this scenario is that the chariot will not make any progress as long as the two horses are pulling in opposite directions.

The key to controlling the desires and emotions that drive us is not to eliminate one or both of the horses. The goal is not to cut ourselves off from our desires and emotions. If we did that, we wouldn't have anything to propel us toward our goals. Instead, the key is to bring your desires and emotions into alignment so that they pull in the same direction. In Plato's analogy, the person driving the chariot—the charioteer—represents the intellect or reason. It is the job of your intellect to control your desires and emotions by guiding them so they work *for* you instead of *against* you.

When your desires are aligned, your emotion becomes the horsepower that pulls you in the direction you want to go. Most of our lives look a lot like a chariot that is out of control. Our desires fight and pull in opposite directions. As a result, the chariot is yanked this way and that. There is no clear sense of direction, and the charioteer is hanging on for dear life. Just imagine if you were able to bring those horses into alignment. Imagine if, instead of hanging on for dear life, *you* were in charge of the direction you're going. Simply learning to align your desires can be the difference between accomplishing next to nothing in your life and accomplishing your wildest dreams.

This might sound good, but it can be hard to see how to do it. So, let's take the analogy of the chariot a bit further than Plato did. The reason Plato's analogy works is because it is based in reality. Not only do we all recognize that there are competing desires inside each one of us, but we also know that it is incredibly difficult to get two horses to pull in the exact same direction. There are two main things that people have traditionally done in order to get two horses to run together. First, they use a yoke. They attach the horses together so that they aren't able to pull in opposite directions. And, second, they put blinders on the horses so they can only look straight ahead.

Both of these tactics make it much easier for the charioteer to steer the horses. On the one hand, yoking them together makes it impossible for them to run in two different directions. And, on the other hand, putting blinders on their eyes makes it impossible for them to aim at anything that's not straight ahead. With these tactics in place, the charioteer simply has to worry about two things: making sure the chariot is always pointed in the right direction, and ensuring that his horses are healthy and running as fast as they can.

In psychological terms, these tactics are referred to as "forcing functions." Forcing functions are the things we put in place to help "force" either ourselves or others to take specific actions. The yoke and blinders are forcing functions for horses because they eliminate the possibility of the horses doing anything but what the charioteer wants them to do: run straight ahead.

There are millions of different forcing functions we can use in our own lives to help align our desires. Working in an environment where you won't be distracted by your phone or your family, disabling the internet on your computer when you're working, taking the plate of cookies off the counter, and making a strict rule that you're not allowed to brood on past offenses are all examples of forcing functions. These kinds of forcing functions are akin to putting blinders on yourself because they effectively put the things that will distract you from your goals out of sight. If you can't focus on them, you will be much less likely to want to run towards them. The exact habits you need to focus on in your life will depend entirely on your own situation and what you're pursuing.

Similarly, there are many examples of forcing functions you can use to effectively yoke your desires together. These forcing functions include anything that helps to keep you running in the right direction. For example, if you marry someone who is strong and willing to challenge you, you will make it difficult for your desire for control to hijack your desire for love. As a result, your partner will help you form a loving relationship that doesn't degenerate into a power game. And that will be better for you in the long run. Again, if you choose to take a job where you know you'll be challenged, rather than a job where you can make an easy paycheck, you have yoked yourself to something that will help to propel you forward. You will benefit far more from the development of character and skills required by a challenging job than you will from an easy job. Again, how this works in your life will depend on your exact situation.

The extent to which you are able to align your desires will depend on how well you guide them with your intellect. Using forcing functions is the first and simplest way you can start to do this. But being able to regulate your emotion is vitally important as well. This is like the charioteer's ability to use the reins to steer the horses, speed them up, and slow them down. Learning to regulate your emotions is not as simple as using forcing functions. It requires that you constantly work to gain a big-picture perspective. Thankfully, if you follow the other laws in this book, you will find that you are able to regulate your emotions more easily because you will have the perspective needed to react appropriately to the things that you experience.

Using forcing functions, coupled with a growing ability to regulate your emotions, will naturally bring your desires into greater alignment. You will find that you won't have wild swings of emotion as each desire takes turns pulling in the direction it wants to go. And, when your desires are pulling in the same direction, you can go really fast.

So, what are some things you can implement today that will help you bring your desires and emotions into alignment?

39. The Law of Internal Dialogue

Every cell is eavesdropping on your internal dialogue.
—Deepak Chopra

The Law of Internal Dialogue states that success requires positive self-talk. This is because you are your most important supporter. If the world is against you but you continue to support yourself, you will succeed. Conversely, if the world supports you but you let your own inner dialogue stand in your way, you will not succeed.

I used to laugh at people who recommended positive self-talk. The idea that you can find success just by sending yourself positive messages sounded a little hokey to me. But then I did some research. As it turns out, studies have shown that self-talk is real. And it's very important. This is because what you say to yourself about your abilities, personality, gifts and weaknesses determines your core identity. It determines how you understand who you are. And, what you think about who you are directly impacts how you behave.

We all have self-talk that reinforces positive or negative thoughts. This self-talk is so immediate and natural that most of the time we aren't even aware that it's going on in our heads. So, stop and think for a minute. What do you say to yourself when you make a mistake? Do you blame yourself? Do you call yourself an idiot? Do you blame others? Do you think of yourself as a victim? How do you react when something unexpected happens? What about when you accomplish something positive? How often do you say to yourself that you "can't" do something? How often do you think that you won't achieve what you want because you don't deserve it? If you pay attention to the thoughts that involuntarily flash through your mind, you will begin to notice patterns. And these patterns will usually be either positive or negative.

Unfortunately, a lot of us have developed patterns of negative self-talk. When we make a mistake, we blame ourselves. We get mad at ourselves. We get embarrassed with ourselves. When something good happens, we don't want to believe it so we immediately brace for something bad, or we tell ourselves it was a fluke. By developing negative patterns of self-talk, we become our own greatest adversaries because we train our brains to work against our success. We like to think that other people are the ones waiting to tear us down, but, in reality, most of us do it to ourselves. We sabotage our success before we can ever even get going.

The problem with negative self-talk is not only that it makes you feel bad. The real problem is that it prevents you from accomplishing your goals. Obviously, telling yourself that you don't deserve success or that you don't have what it takes to be successful isn't good for your sense of belief. But, saying things like this to yourself also confuses your brain. Remember, your brain cannot distinguish between images that you don't want to think about and those you do want to think about. Recall how I mentioned when discussing the Law of Focus that, if I told you not to think about an orange pig, an image of an orange pig will automatically pop into your mind. Well, the same principle is at work here: speaking negatively to yourself about yourself feeds your brain with images of you failing or not being good enough.

The more you feed these negative thoughts about yourself to your brain, the more time your brain spends thinking about them. And the more time your brain spends thinking about these thoughts, the more your attention gets diverted from focusing on success. If you recall the Law of Focus, you will remember that you will start to move in the direction of whatever you focus on most in your life. This means that, when you develop negative patterns of self-talk, it won't take long before you start pursuing failure. When you constantly tell yourself that you don't deserve success, or that you're not as good as other people, your brain takes these thoughts as instructions, and it begins to guide you in ways that will make failure your reality.

The truth is that, in practice, self-talk isn't always this straightforward. Sometimes it is. But, a lot of the time, self-talk is more complicated. You see, our minds have many different perspectives, some of them positive and some of them negative. Each of these perspectives is important, if we want to be able to make informed, mature decisions every day. Just like how it is important for a company to hire people that bring different perspectives to the table in order to succeed, so also the different perspectives in your own head help you make the best decisions you possibly can. Every time you make a decision there is a dialogue inside your head about what you should do. Sometimes this dialogue happens fast—so fast you might not even notice it. Other times, the dialogue can take a long time. Most of us probably don't spend much time debating with ourselves whether we should eat a banana. We simply see it, pick it up, and eat it. We certainly don't spend as much time deciding whether to eat a banana as we do trying to decide whether to make an offer on a new home, for example. You might spend hours or days mulling over a big decision like that. However, despite not noticing it, there is still a dialogue that takes place even when deciding to eat a banana. There will be a little voice telling you to do it, and a little voice telling you to grab a cookie instead. You might not notice it, but it's there, along with a number of other little voices.

When you reinforce negative thoughts about yourself or your abilities, you give power to the voices that represent negative perspectives in your head. If you're constantly telling yourself that you don't deserve to be happy, or that you're not smart, you're effectively telling your brain to raise the volume on the voices that represent negative perspectives just a little bit. Now, every time an internal dialogue takes place, whether it's about eating a banana, buying a new home, or something else entirely, you start to hear the negative voices just a bit more. The more negative information you feed your brain, the louder those voices become. Eventually, when you know that you need to go to bed in order to ensure that you'll be in the best state of mind for work in the morning, you find yourself watching one more episode of your favorite show. That little voice in your inner dialogue telling you to stay up has become so loud that you can't ignore it any longer. It tells you that you don't need to go to bed. So, you stay up. Where did that voice come from? In truth, it has always been there; it's one of your many perspectives constantly engaged in a dialogue in your head. The difference is that, by feeding your brain negative information about yourself, you've allowed that voice to become louder than the other voices in your head.

The good thing is that this law works the other way around as well. It's not just the negative voices that get louder; you can make the positive voices louder, too. Every time you engage in *positive* self-talk, you help to silence the negative voices in your head and allow the positive voices to get louder. Then, instead of only hearing a voice telling you to stay up for one more episode, you'll hear a much louder voice telling you to go to bed because you actually believe that it matters if you're at your best tomorrow.

Which do you think will lead to more success? Obviously, reinforcing the positive voice.

Just like with any of the laws in this book, there's no special formula that will automatically make you good at managing your internal dialogue. The first step is paying attention to the dialogue happening in your head. Then, make the decision to start giving your brain positive information to work with—information that will take you toward your goals instead of blocking your way.

40. The Law of Adjustment

It is not the strongest that survive, nor the most
intelligent, but the most responsive to change.
—Charles Darwin

The Law of Adjustment states that success depends on
continual course correction. We've all heard that the
shortest distance between two points is a straight line.
And that's true. But, in practice, the path to success will
never be a straight line. It will always have twists and turns.
There will always be outside forces that push you off course.
The key to success, then, is not staying on course 100% of
the time; the key is to be able to bring yourself back on
course every time you drift off.

If you're anything like me, whenever you're on a long
flight you probably spend a fair bit of time tracking the
plane's progress on that little screen on the chair in front of
you. It's a helpful little map to see how far the plane has
gone, how close you are to your destination, and if you might
be flying over anything particularly interesting. According
to this screen, the flight path is always a straight line. It is
the most direct route. And the plane follows this straight line
exactly—or so it seems.

Did you know that, in reality, an airplane is only exactly on course about 10% of the time? It's true. The vast majority of the time, the plane is actually off course. Wind, air pressure, and human error are just some of the reasons why the plane floats off course constantly. Contrary to what most of us assume, the pilot's job is not to keep the airplane flying in a straight line because that's impossible. The pilot's job is to constantly make small adjustments that bring the drifting plane back on course.

Below is a visual of a planned flight path versus the actual flight path. The straight line is the planned flight path, and the curvy line is the actual path the plane takes.

If you add up the time the plane is actually on course, it only comes to about 10% of the flight, which means that the plane arrives at its destination having been off course for 90% of the flight.

If the pilot did not correct the plane's course every time, the route would look more like this:

Obviously, it would be pretty difficult for the plane to arrive at its intended destination without the pilot making continual adjustments.

Success in any area of life almost always looks a lot like this. Psychologists have actually mapped what the average path to any goal looks like, and it's even more varied than a plane's flightpath:

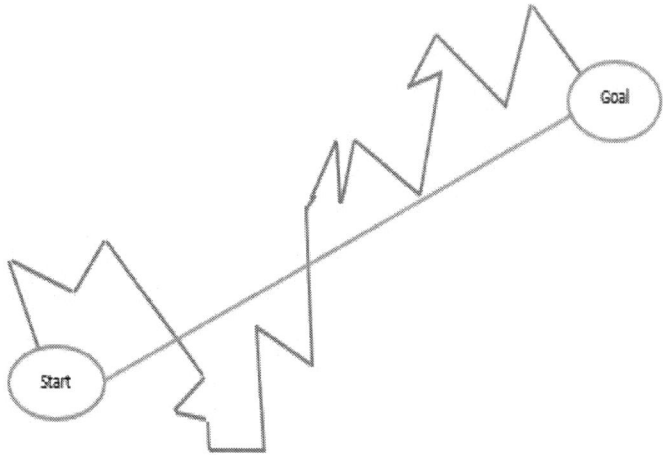

The lesson here is that you should not expect to achieve any significant goal in your life by following the most direct path. Yes, it is still important to *try* to follow the most direct path because that will ensure that your course corrections get you where you want to go in the end. But you should also recognize that you *will* veer off course.

If you look closely at the path to goal achievement above, you will notice that the average trajectory of success includes *not* being on course at any point along the journey. Think about that for a minute. How many times have you given up on something because it seemed like you couldn't make progress or couldn't stay on track? Did you ever stop to think that you might have been making the exact right amount of progress, even though you were off course the entire time?

Now, while it's true that you should not expect your path to success to follow the most direct route, this does not mean that you can do away with that direct route altogether. Just because an airplane doesn't follow the intended flightpath exactly doesn't mean that it doesn't still need that flightpath in order to reach its destination. The intended flight path is valuable not because the plane will follow it to a tee, but rather because it provides the information necessary for the pilot to make adjustments. In the same way, it is absolutely essential that you have a plan that serves as the most direct route from where you are today to where you want to be. That plan will be the guide you use to make the adjustments necessary to get you where you want to go.

One thing about the Law of Adjustment that makes it challenging, even once you understand it, is that it can be exhausting. A lot of people start off well. They make the necessary adjustments to correct their course for the first few weeks. But eventually they stop. They get tired of having to always make adjustments. They might decide that the reward is not worth the effort. Other times people think the fact that they can't stay on course means that there's something wrong with them. But that's not true. The truth is that correction never ends. There will always be things that come up that require course corrections. That's the Law of Adjustment at work.

Understanding the Law of Adjustment is vitally important for your success because it allows you to shift your focus from trying to stay on course to making the adjustments when you do veer off course. I constantly meet people frustrated and disappointed in themselves because they cannot seem to stay on track. They think there's something wrong with them or with their plan. They think that they should be on course 100% of the time, and anything less is failure. But this isn't realistic. *Success is never measured by how well you stay on course; it is measured by how well you adjust when you inevitably veer off course.* In the book, *Atomic Habits*, James Clear makes this very point. According to Clear, instead of holding yourself to the impossible standard of being perfect every day, you should hold yourself to the standard of never missing the mark two days in a row: "Never miss twice," he says. The important point is that, in order to have success, you will constantly need to be making adjustments to correct your course. If you can continue to make the necessary adjustments, and if you can do so consistently, you will achieve success.

41. The Law of Generosity

The measure of your success will be the measure of
your generosity.

—John Paul II

T he Law of Generosity states that being generous
breeds success. This law might be the most counter-
intuitive law in this book. On the surface, it seems
like it can't be true. How can you get more by giving more
away? How can you get more time, money, comfort,
meaning, and success by giving what little of those things
you currently have away? Many of us are accustomed to
thinking of the most successful people as being cold and
ruthless, always looking out for themselves. But this isn't
true. You really can get more by giving what you have away.

In order to explain how generosity works, let me tell you
a bit about Adam Grant, a professor of organizational
psychology in the prestigious Wharton School at the
University of Pennsylvania. If anybody knows about
success, it would be him. Grant has an impressive list of
accolades. Eight years ago, when he was just thirty-one years
old, he was awarded tenure, making him the youngest
professor ever to receive that honor at Wharton. Today, at

the age of thirty-nine, he holds the title of Wharton's top-rated professor for seven years running. Over the past decade, he has written five #1 New York Times bestselling books that have been translated into thirty-five different languages, and he has been called upon to consult for a number of impressive companies, including Google, Goldman Sachs, the United Nations, the Gates Foundation, and the NFL. Grant has been recognized as one of the world's ten most influential management thinkers, and he has been named in Fortune Magazine's 40 under 40. He has served on the Defense Innovation Board at the Pentagon, and the World Economic Forum has named him as a Young Global Leader. In addition to all this, his two TED talks have been viewed more than twenty-five million times. Almost any way you measure it, Grant has been successful.

But, according to Grant, the key to success is not selfishness or ruthlessness. Rather, the key to success is being as generous and selfless as possible. In fact, this is what his first best-selling book was all about. In that book, called *Give and Take: A Revolutionary Approach to Success*, Grant reports that his research has revealed that there are three types of people in virtually every workplace: takers, matchers, and givers.

Takers are the people who always have a selfish angle for everything they do. They are always looking out for number one. Most people aren't takers, but there will always be a certain percentage of people in any organization, family, or team, who belong to this category.

According to Grant, the vast majority of people are matchers. Matchers always work to balance the legers. When a matcher asks for a favor from a colleague, he automatically feels a responsibility to repay that favor, and vice versa. If the matcher is being paid for eight hours, she will work up until that time and no further. Matchers are usually happy to help out their colleagues, but they always expect that, at some point in the future, the colleague will return the favor.

But then there are givers. Givers have no expectation of reciprocity. Givers tirelessly pitch in to help their colleagues and friends succeed without ever expecting anything in return. They always put others' interests above their own.

Grant's research found that takers often succeed in the short-term, but they almost never succeed in the long-term. This is because they always get found out and, as studies have shown, most of us want to punish people we perceive to be takers, even if it means that we have to sacrifice some of our own success in the process. Knowing this, it makes sense that it's only a matter of time before takers are pushed back down the ladder of success.

Matchers, on the other hand, don't typically do enough to achieve much success. They typically don't take risks and they tend to leave a transactional impression on the people they work with. Most people don't like working with colleagues that are keeping score, even if they are keeping score themselves. The positive thing about matchers is that they usually let their colleagues know where they stand. This usually earns them enough respect to rise beyond the lowest ranks. But, because they always work to keep an even score, they don't usually earn any extra credit from anyone, which typically means that they are stuck meddling in the middle.

As you might expect, Grant's research found that there are a disproportionate number of givers at the bottom of any organization. These people are so busy helping other people that their own productivity ends up being pretty dismal. They don't succeed because they're too busy helping other people. This makes sense. It's what most of us would probably expect to find.

But Grant's research also revealed something that was very unexpected. He found that, not only are there typically a disproportionate number of givers at the bottom of any organization, but there are also a disproportionate number of givers who climb all the way to the top, far exceeding all their peers. So, while takers and matchers tend to make up the average worker, givers tend to be congregated at the very bottom and at the very top.

Grant found that there are some key differences between the givers that achieve wild success and those that stack up on the bottom. In particular, givers who achieve success do so by setting healthy boundaries, while those for whom success remains elusive fail to do this. This means that, while givers of all stripes routinely do favors for colleagues without any strings attached, successful givers are careful not to overextend themselves to the point where they sacrifice their own career goals. Specifically, Grant found that successful givers tend to help everyone they can by committing a little time to each person, while givers at the bottom typically devote more time to helping fewer people. As a result, the givers at the bottom spend all their time helping other people succeed at the expense of their own success, while those who rise to the top are able to express high levels of generosity to a wide range of people while remaining highly productive themselves.

By setting boundaries, successful givers harness the power of the Law of Generosity and use it to their advantage. As a result, they tend to construct networks of people who appreciate their value. Their colleagues perceive them as selfless and free from ulterior motives, but *also* as productive contributors to the shared mission. Furthermore, because they share credit without demanding any in return, colleagues are eager to work with givers and supervisors look forward to giving them new opportunities. In general, people tend to be less skeptical of ideas that come from givers, and so their projects tend to actually get done more often than is the case with takers and matchers. This is a huge benefit that givers with boundaries are able to take advantage of. Givers with healthy boundaries usually develop a positive reputation, and their accumulation of grateful colleagues eventually grows to the point where positive effects become inevitable. As a result, these givers create positive feedback loops that push them further and further up the ladder of success.

In a profile of Grant run in the *New York Times Magazine* a number of years ago, he showed that he practices what he preaches. His core strategy for success in his own life is to be as generous and selfless as possible. And he credits that commitment for all the success he has enjoyed so far in his life.

One of the most difficult lessons to learn when it comes to the Law of Generosity is that success is not a zero-sum game. It is *not* true that the more success you have the less someone else has to have. It is *not* true that there must be winners and losers. It's *not* as if we all share a big success pizza and every time someone takes a slice, there are fewer slices left for everyone else. It can be easy to think that this is how it is. But it's not true.

As Grant's research has shown, success works the other way around. The more generous you are, the more success is available for everyone. It's as if every time you take a slice from the big success pizza and give it to someone else, two additional slices magically appear. So, don't be afraid to be generous. In fact, if you're not already a giver, I dare you to become one. If you do, you will soon see that success becomes inevitable.

42. The Law of Gratitude

Gratitude is not only the greatest of virtues, but the parent of all the others.

—Cicero

The Law of Gratitude states that being grateful improves both the amount and quality of success one can achieve. Self-help gurus have been saying this for years, but there is now some substantial scientific evidence to back this up. Numerous studies have now shown that practicing gratitude increases at least your happiness, your ability to work with others, your level of motivation, your sense of worth, and your overall life satisfaction. Gratitude is also the single most important factor for determining generosity, and it has been shown to have an impact on physical well-being as well. This makes gratitude one of the most powerful determinants of well-being and success that we know of.

Put in technical terms, gratitude is a positive emotion that you experience when you perceive that someone has intentionally given you a valuable benefit of some kind. And we know that experiencing positive emotion not only impacts your well-being, but it can have a dramatic impact on your productivity as well. The more positive emotion and less anxiety you experience, the more productive you will be. You will be able to concentrate better, think more clearly, and focus your attention more accurately. Most importantly, you will be happier. Studies have repeatedly shown that happiness has a direct correlation with increased productivity. The happier you are, the more productive you will be. And the more productive you are, the higher the level of success you can usually achieve. Gratitude is one of the best ways we know of to increase our happiness beyond a superficial level.

The thing about gratitude, however, is that it cannot be manufactured. There is no "gratitude hack," despite what some people might say. In other words, you must actually *be* grateful in order to reap the benefits of gratitude. Furthermore, gratitude cannot be experienced without other people. It is what is known as an "interpersonal emotion," which means that it cannot be directed toward yourself; it must be directed toward others. And, the more specific you make your object of gratitude, the more you will benefit from it.

What this means is that, to use the Law of Gratitude to your advantage, you need to cultivate a sincere sense of gratitude toward actual people for genuine acts. A lot of people talk about cultivating gratitude by simply writing down a handful of things you're grateful for each day. They say that you can be thankful for the weather and for your family. But, while this will have some effect on your overall expression of gratitude, it won't really tap into the power of gratitude. Gratitude is a deep emotion. Its effects cannot be simulated by thinking about surface-level features in your life that you're "grateful" for.

If you really want to cultivate gratitude in your life, you need to reverse engineer the contexts that produce gratitude and then focus on fostering and recognizing those contexts. Many psychologists believe that there are three major requirements for an expression of gratitude. First, you must have received a gift or outcome that you value from an actual person. Second, you must have received it at some cost to the person giving you the outcome. Third, the benefit must have been given with benevolent intentions, not in an attempt to do you harm or because they had an obligation of some kind. So, to say you are thankful for your family is nice, but it's hard to see who "gave" them to you, how it cost that person anything, or how that gift was benevolent. Cultivating genuine gratitude requires a bit more effort on your part.

Taking the three key elements of gratitude as our cue, however, there is a much better way to foster more gratitude in your life: simply take a few minutes to walk through each of the three steps every day. Did you receive an outcome that you valued today? Did someone give you a chocolate bar? Did you receive a word of encouragement? Did somebody give you a gift? The answer will almost certainly be yes. Most of us will receive *something* from someone else every day. If you can't think of at least ten things, you're probably not thinking hard enough.

Then, once you've thought about all the valuable things you've received from others in the day, think about what it cost for the people to give you those gifts. Did they have to give up their own time or pay for something from their own pocket? There are many different ways people can incur a cost, so be sure to think long and hard about this one.

Then, once you've thought through the costs involved, think for a while about their intentions. Why did the people give you gifts in the first place? Is it because they care about your success? Do they value you as a friend? Do they love you as their family member?

Writing your answers to each of these three elements down will naturally unlock gratitude in your heart, and all the benefits that go along with it. As you continue to cultivate gratitude in your life, the benefits increase as well. So far as we can tell, there is no limit to the benefit gratitude has in our lives. There is no point where you will "max out." So, if you want the benefits, push yourself to experience more and more gratitude.

43. The Law of Honesty

Honesty and transparency make you vulnerable. Be honest and transparent anyway.

—Mother Teresa

The Law of Honesty states that success requires the truth. If you want to have success of any kind, you need to be as honest as possible with yourself. And, if you want to have long-term success, you cannot deceive other people, either.

In his book, *The (Honest) Truth About Dishonesty*, Dan Ariely explains that the vast majority of us believe that we're honest, even though we all lie and cheat in small ways. We believe we're honest because we're only dishonest in ways that we think don't matter. We convince ourselves that a small lie here and a little deception there isn't really a big deal. After all, we're not hurting anyone, right? According to Ariely, the vast majority of people in the world believe that they're fundamentally honest; but almost nobody is actually as honest as they think.

Most often, we lie to avoid suffering painful consequences that we think will result from telling the truth. It's quite common to tell little lies to avoid being embarrassed, for example, or to avoid conflict, or to save ourselves from earning a tarnished reputation. Nobody likes to feel pain or be put in an uncomfortable situation, especially if it might impact the way people think of us. So, if there's a way to avoid pain while also protecting our image, you can bet that we'll try to take it every single time.

Other times, we lie to try to get things we want. We all know someone who exaggerates every story they tell. We know before they open their mouth that what's about to come out will only be partially true. And they might even know that we know this. But they do it anyway. They do it because they want attention. They like to see the reaction people have when they tell their stories. They like the fact that all eyes are on them, even if they know that most people aren't going to believe them. They tell the lie because it gets them something they want.

But, while we might roll our eyes at our friend who exaggerates every story, we are all guilty of telling lies when we think it will help to get us something we want. If we think that a small lie will bring us more money, power, affection, or chocolate cake, it's likely that we'll tell it. It is predictable human behavior. That's why we react so strongly when we see conflicts of interest in action. We know that people— including ourselves—will stretch the truth more often than not if we think it will help us get what we want.

This isn't only the case when it comes to deceiving others, either. We are constantly faced with temptations to deceive ourselves as well. When we don't get the job we had our hearts set on, we tell ourselves that we didn't really want it anyway. When we give in to the temptation of scrolling through social media instead of doing productive work, we justify it by telling ourselves that we deserve a break. When we fight with a friend, we convince ourselves that they aren't smart or kind, and that we are beyond reproach. When we get dumped, we tell ourselves that it's their loss. Every day we are faced with thousands of temptations to deceive ourselves. Some are big and some are small. And a lot of the time we give in.

Perhaps the biggest lie we tell ourselves is that all the little lies don't matter. Because they certainly do. No matter how innocent you might think a little half-truth might be, the one thing you can say for sure is that it does matter. Sure, it might be true that a little exaggeration or subtle omission won't make a big difference in the lives of your friends or family. But each time you choose to lie to avoid something you don't want or to get something you do want, it makes a huge difference in *your* life.

Let me explain. Telling the truth is very often inconvenient. It's hard. It can create difficult situations that could be easily avoided with a lie or two. But, as we've already learned from numerous other laws in this book, these difficult situations are actually the opportunities you need in order to enhance your character, skills, and abilities. This means that every time you tell a lie, whether to yourself or to someone else, you prevent yourself from becoming the person you could be. When you lie, you're pretending to be someone you wish you were; when you tell the truth, especially when it's inconvenient, you're taking steps to become that person in real life.

And here's why the Law of Honesty is one of the Laws of Success: more often than not, the person you could be is a person who would have more success than you currently enjoy. You see, every time you face an opportunity to lie, you are standing at a crossroads. One way will almost certainly lead to long-term success, and the other way will lead to long-term failure. You can pretend to be the person that you have not yet become—the person who will achieve long-term success. You can pretend to be smart, right, respected, kind, or diligent. Whenever you tell a lie to yourself or someone else, you are pretending to be someone you aren't. Your other option is to not pretend. Taking this option is not always fun. In the short term, you might lose friends, miss out on opportunities, or look stupid. But these experiences show you the exact things you need to work on. They tell you where you need to improve, if you want to have success. Telling the truth becomes your compass for success because it points you in the exact direction you need to go.

But it gets even better. Not only will telling the truth *point* you in the right direction; telling the truth will *push* you in that direction, too. You see, our brains don't like contradictions. They don't like it when what we see and what we believe are at odds. They don't like it when what we want is not our reality. When this happens, we experience what is called cognitive dissonance. And our brains work as hard as possible to resolve this dissonance. One of the most common ways our brains try to resolve the dissonance is to present a lie to us. If we believe a lie, we can resolve the dissonance. If, for example, you're not as smart as you'd like to be, you will find yourself constantly faced with opportunities to make yourself sound smarter than you really are. This is your brain's way of trying to resolve the dissonance between who you are and who you want to be. Your brain suggests that you tell a lie because that's the easy way to resolve this dissonance. When you lie, you don't have to worry about putting in all the hard work it takes to get smarter. You simply pretend to be who you desperately wish you were.

But, if you refuse to accept lies, your brain will spur you on to resolve the dissonance in another way: it will push you to actually change your behavior.

247

However, before it does this, it will first try one last-ditch effort to get you to accept a lie. If you will not pretend to be smarter than you really are, for example, your brain will soon learn that it cannot resolve the dissonance by presenting simple lies to you. So, it will present you with a different, much more subtle kind of lie. It will try to change your ideal. It will tell you that you don't actually *want* to be smarter. It will try to convince you to give up on your ideal.

However, if you are committed to being honest with yourself, you will not accept this lie either. Just like how you will doggedly refuse to pretend you're smarter than you really are, so also you must take a stand against disappearing your ideal.

And here, after all this hard, psychological work, is where the magic kicks in. When your brain realizes that you will not allow it to solve the dissonance by lying, it will turn to the only other option. It will push you to solve it by being truthful. At this point, it's like your brain has given up and resigned itself to the fact that the only way to resolve the dissonance is to get down to doing the hard work of actually becoming smarter. If you refuse to pretend you're smarter than you really are, and you refuse to believe lies about your ideal, your brain will begin to push you to become smarter. You'll find that you become just a little more motivated to read books, listen to podcasts, or watch lectures. It will naturally push you to become the person you wish you were.

Telling the truth in every area of life is not easy. But it's worth it. In the short term, you will experience pain, rejection, and possibly shame. But, over time, not only will you become a better person, but you will also find that your relationships become more meaningful, your customers are more loyal, your peers have more respect for you, and you are given opportunities that are ten times better than the ones you might have lost out on. When people learn that they can trust you, they will treat you differently. You will become their go-to person for the most valuable and important things.

But, what's especially important is that, when you know that you're honest, you will treat yourself differently. You will carry yourself differently. You will have more respect for yourself, and you will have more confidence because you have nothing to hide. Thomas Jefferson once said, "Honesty is the first chapter in the book of wisdom." And he was right. In order to grow into a long-term success, honesty is essential.

But honesty isn't just about long-term rewards. When you commit to being honest with yourself and with others, you will find that it brings more immediate results as well. You will find that you are much more aware of where you are succeeding and where you can improve. Instead of allowing your brain to explain away the myriad of mistakes you inevitably make every day, you will force yourself to confront them head on. This isn't always fun, but it will drastically improve your rate of success across every domain of life. As James Altucher has said, "Honesty is the fastest way to prevent a mistake from turning into a failure." So, not only will honesty bring you long-term benefits of character development; it will also bring you more immediate results, too.

Dishonesty is a funny thing. It's like a weed that grows really fast. As soon as you allow yourself to be dishonest in one area of your life, you will find it much easier to be dishonest in other areas of your life as well. It's like your brain is just waiting for you to give it the green light. And once you allow it to take the route of dishonesty once, it now knows that that's an acceptable option. That is why you cannot try to be honest in one area of your life and not in other areas. It won't work. If you want to harness the power of the Law of Honesty, you need to be honest in every area of your life. As it turns out, the old saying is true: honesty really is the best policy.

44. The Law of the Snowball

A miracle is when the whole is greater than the sum of its parts. A miracle is when one plus one equals a thousand.

—Frederick Buechner

The Law of the Snowball states that success will exceed the sum of its parts, *if* you are persistent. If you're anything like 99.9% of the population, there are probably days when you struggle to get through the grind. There are days when you feel like you aren't making much of a difference and you doubt whether you are making any progress toward your goals at all. According to the Law of the Snowball, these days—the days when you feel like giving up—are the days that really count. Because these are the days where one plus one can equal a thousand.

Everybody has days when they *feel* motivated. Everybody has days when things just seem to work out and when the creativity juices flow freely. These are great days, and they should be celebrated. But everybody has them. Everybody thinks that they make progress on these days.

What separates those who achieve success from those who don't is that successful people recognize that the days when they will make real progress are the days when they feel like they're banging their head against a brick wall over and over again. On those days—the days when inspiration is on vacation—unsuccessful people give up. But successful people keep on banging away. It's ugly. It's not fun. But it's necessary.

If you were to turn all the times you bang your head against your proverbial brick wall into a math equation, adding each hit you've taken, blow by blow, the sum of your equation should be a concussion. But, miraculously, that's not what happens. When you look back on the days when everything feels effortless and it seems that the universe has conspired to fulfill all your deepest desires, the math equation usually adds up. It is usually plainly obvious how your actions brought about your results—at least that's how it looks. But on the tough days (which are often much more numerous, by the way) the math rarely adds up. When you look back on those days, you will always find that your results on those days have exceeded the sum of the parts.

The secret of this law is the compounding principle, which means that little, seemingly insignificant, actions taken today will compound into massive results in a year from now, or even ten years from now. You can think of every little action you take like a snowball you roll down a hill. The more actions you take, the more snowballs you have rolling down the hill. As these snowballs roll down to the bottom, they pick up more and more snow. By the time they reach the bottom, they are much bigger than they were when you initially formed them.

This is especially true for the actions you take on the days where it feels like you're not making any progress. All day, you're rolling little snowballs down a hill, and you only feel like you're not making any progress because none of those snowballs have reached the bottom yet. But they will. It might take so long that you forget that you rolled them in the first place. But they will eventually reach the bottom. And, when they do, they will be much, much bigger than they were when you initially rolled them.

It's impossible to know exactly how much snow each snowball will pick up. It's possible that reading a chapter of a book on ancient spirituality, for example, will end up helping you lose thirty pounds. You won't know. Reading that chapter might cause you to think of yourself just a little bit differently, which increases your self-esteem ever so slightly. This, in turn, changes how you look at yourself and how you think about physical health. You begin eating healthier foods. You begin to feel a connection with nature, which could help to inspire you to get out and go for a walk every day. Before you know it, the thirty pounds you've been wanting to shed for years is suddenly falling off your body, and, for some people, this can be truly transforming.

But the snowball might roll further. Reading that chapter might help you lose weight, which, in turn, might improve your self-esteem, which could increase your energy-levels, which will make you feel more motivated, which will make you perform better at work, which might earn you the recognition of your colleagues, which will earn you that promotion you've been eying.

You simply do not know how big each snowball will get by the time it reaches the bottom of the hill. You do not know which actions will conspire to produce which results. And, in retrospect, you probably will never be able to tell, either. But, what you can be sure of is that each snowball will reach the bottom.

At the risk of pushing the snowball analogy too far, let me briefly explain the three main reasons why the Law of the Snowball is so important on the days where you feel like packing it in.

First of all, the snowballs you make on tough days tend to be bigger when they reach the bottom than the snowballs you make on good days. This is because they require more energy to make. In other words, because every action you take on the days when you feel like giving up requires more effort, you end up putting more into everything you do. What this means is that, on bad days, you often end up doing a better job than you do on good days. You almost certainly do more of the right things in the right way than you do on good days, even if it doesn't feel like it. On good days, when everything is flowing, there isn't as much effort needed. And, when you don't put as much effort into your actions, they will bring smaller results in the long run. It feels good when things seem effortless. But always remember: the bigger the effort at the top, the bigger the result at the bottom.

Second, by pushing through and rolling snowballs down the hill on days when you don't feel like it, you have more snowballs rolling at any time than the people who give up. People who take days off when it's raining or when they feel sick don't get snowballs on those days. Therefore, they have fewer snowballs rolling down the hill at any one time. It's simple math: the more often you roll snowballs down the hill, the more snowballs will accumulate at the bottom. Or, to put it another way, the more actions you take, the more results you will have. So, not only do your results on difficult days tend to be of better quality, but they also add up to be of greater quantity.

Finally, by showing up every day, rain or shine, and taking consistent action toward your goals, you avoid making destructive snowballs that will end up preventing you from making progress even on the good days. You see, the Law of the Snowball is not only at work when it comes to making positive progress; it is also at work in the opposite direction as well. The truth is that there is a snowball for *each* action you take, good or bad. So, sleeping in instead of getting up and getting to work is also a snowball you roll down the hill. But, instead of accumulating snow, it's destructive. It takes snow away from the other snowballs as it bounces into them. In other words, it works against you. Every time you don't show up, you roll a destructive snowball down your hill. Every time you take the easy way out, you roll a destructive snowball down your hill. Every time you quit, you roll a destructive snowball down your hill. Not only do these destructive snowballs not help you succeed, but they actively work against your success by reducing the size of all your other snowballs. When you show up and do the right things on the tough days, then, you don't just gain an advantage; you avoid giving yourself a disadvantage.

When you put these three factors together, it becomes clear how harnessing the power of the Law of the Snowball will lead to truly staggering results. When you consistently show up on the tough days and work through the pain, you will eventually have four, five, or ten times the results of those who don't. Yes, you will have put in more time and effort, but your results will still be disproportionate. You won't put in four or five times as much effort. Yet, you'll get at least four or five times the results. Looking back, you will have found that you've made one plus one equal a thousand. And that's a miracle.

45. The Law of Seasons

Success is very largely a matter of adjusting one's self to the ever-varying and changing environments of life, in a spirit of harmony and poise.

—Napoleon Hill

The Law of Seasons states that success requires the ability to take advantage of opportunities that come from changing circumstances. Success is not a static state; it is not something you accomplish and then move on. This means that, in order to have success, you need to be able to manage your journey differently in different seasons of life. This will, inevitably, require different skills and abilities from you.

I have had the opportunity to live in some different places throughout my life. By far, my favorite places to live are those places where there are four distinct seasons each year: spring, summer, fall, and winter. I love it because each season has its own beauty. I love it when the snow starts to melt in the spring because it feels like the whole world is waking up after a long nap. Birds are chirping, trees are leafing out, and tulips are popping out of the ground. I love summer, when you can sit with friends on a patio or go to the beach or go hiking. I think fall is probably my favorite season. There's just something about seeing the leaves on the trees start turning all the different shades of yellow, orange, and red, as they begin to fall to the ground. I don't know what it is; I just like the way it makes me feel. But I also love winter. The crunch of fresh snow beneath my feet, the feeling of taking a deep breath of cold air, and seeing the moon, reflecting off the blanket of white snow on the ground, brighten up the night. There are so many great winter activities, too. From hiking to snowshoeing, skiing to ice fishing, it's like we enter a whole new world in the winter. It's amazing.

But each season also brings distinct challenges. For example, where I currently live, the spring season brings flooding. As the snow melts, the rivers and creeks rise, overflow their banks and threaten to fill thousands of homes with water. Inevitably, there will be some unlucky homeowners each year who are displaced for a few weeks until the threat of flooding subsides. In the summer, it can get so dry that fires become a real danger, and water advisories prevent people from watering their lawns. Once again, these fires pose a serious risk to people's homes and livelihoods each year. Then, in the fall, we tend to get a lot of rain and wind. This can wreak havoc by causing power outages and toppled trees. But all of this is nothing compared to what we deal with in the winter. Winter often brings blizzards that make it impossible to go anywhere or do just about anything, and weather so cold that bare skin will freeze in less than two minutes. It's a beautiful place to live, but it's also challenging.

There are a lot of people that live here who use the climate to make a living. There are companies who specialize in flood repair, fire prevention, or snow removal.

Other companies provide recreational services built around the seasons. Because of the different seasons, there is quite a range of opportunities people can take advantage of to make a living. And that's great.

As with any city, there are some companies that are extremely successful, some that are only moderately successful, and quite a few that are constantly operating on the brink of bankruptcy. Given all the opportunities provided by the seasons, I find it curious that some companies are still having trouble staying in business. Many of these struggling companies are operated by smart, competent, honest people. Why are they having such trouble making a go of it in what appears to be the land of opportunity?

I wondered about this for a while until I noticed a pattern. I realized that the difference between the companies who enjoy a high level of success and those who are on the brink of shuttering is actually very simple: the companies enjoying success are able to adapt their services or products to different seasons, whereas the companies struggling aren't able to figure out a way to do this. For example, a company that specializes in flood repair and also offers snow removal services can have business year-round, whereas a company only specializing in flood repair will have a tough time finding clients during the long winter months. Similarly, stores that carry specialized sporting equipment for winter sports as well as summer sports do much better than those who build their reputation by focusing on one or the other. There are different challenges and different opportunities in every season. The companies who do well recognize this, and they see opportunities in each new challenge.

Of course, we don't all live in a place with such extreme weather, but we do all face shifting circumstances in our lives. The question is: how well do you adapt?

While the seasons of the year are relatively predictable, the changing seasons of our lives are slightly less so. I remember meeting one client, Sherry, who came to me exasperated and defeated because every time she thought she had things under control, the season would change and she would have to find a whole new way of pursuing her goal. She was married with three young children, worked a demanding corporate job, and was trying to start a small business on the side. She explained to me in detail how she had tried to squeeze in as much time as possible to get everything done. Given everything she had to do during her day, she knew that the only time she would have to work on her business was first thing in the morning before she headed off to work. She started getting up at 5 a.m. This gave her two hours to work on her business before her husband and kids got up at 7. She did this for a few months and was really making progress. But then her youngest child for some reason started getting up at 6 a.m., instead of 7. He was loud, which meant that her husband woke up as well. Having both of them up made it difficult for her to get anything done after 6 o'clock. She tried to adjust her son's bedtime, but nothing seemed to work.

So, in order to get her two hours in, she adjusted. She started putting in one hour in the evening after the kids were in bed, and then another hour in the morning before everyone got up. But she found this system didn't work. She found that she either had so much to do to prepare for the next day, or she was just so tired that she wasn't making much progress during her hour working on her business in the evening.

So, she pivoted again. This time, she decided to try getting up at 4 a.m. to get her time in. No sooner had she just got into her new routine, and her oldest two kids started playing sports. This meant that, given their new weekly schedules, she couldn't count on being home and in bed early enough to get up at 4 a.m. during the week. If she continued to get up at four o'clock, she could only get five hours of sleep in at most, which wasn't going to be enough.

When I met her, she was ready to give up on her business. She was frustrated that she couldn't seem to find the perfect balance she needed to get everything done. She told me that she was thinking about putting her business on hold until her kids were finished playing sports for the year. As soon as I heard that, I immediately thought about all the business owners I knew that were slowly going bankrupt while they sat idly waiting for the next season to come around. I could see that Sherry was about to join their ranks. She thought she was failing because she had to keep adjusting her approach to the changing circumstances around her. She didn't want the seasons to change in her life. She already knew that she could have success in one particular season, and, out of frustration, she was falling into the trap of thinking that her success was somehow tied to that season. But that's the same logic the snowmobile shop owner uses when he blames his bankruptcy on summer.

As we've already learned in the Law of Adjustment, success cannot be achieved by setting it and forgetting it. Everything is constantly changing. And those who are successful are able to figure out ways to see those changes as new opportunities. I'm happy to say that, eventually, Sherry realized that she was really on the right track the whole time, and she began looking at the constantly changing seasons of her life as an endless series of opportunities. Eventually, she was able to quit her job and work on her business full-time. As far as I can tell, she has never been happier.

Are there times in your life when you violate the Law of Seasons? Are there times when you put off doing something you know you should do because it's "not the right time"? Do you ever find yourself thinking that when circumstances "go back to normal" you'll get back to making progress on your goals? If so, you are violating the Law of Seasons.

Aligning yourself with the Law of Seasons means that, whenever you face a challenge because your circumstances have changed in some way, you'll recognize it as your cue to adjust your approach. Seasons will always be changing in your life, no matter what. Every new season will bring new challenges. That's a guarantee. But it will also bring new opportunities. Your job is to constantly look at how you can overcome the challenges by seizing the opportunities.

46. The Law of Maintenance

Take care of your body. It's the only place you have to live.

—Jim Rohn

The Law of Maintenance states that keeping your health in good shape is essential for success. Just like maintaining a car or a home, your body needs to be taken care of if you want it to last for a long time. And you do want it to last for a long time, because, if it breaks down, that means you break down.

Physical health is a funny thing. Most of us don't think about it all that much. We go about our days, track our calories, make sure we get in our steps, and maybe even hit the gym a couple times a week. But, if we're honest, most of the time we think about our health about as much as someone might think about the glasses sitting on their face.

You see, as long as you're wearing your glasses, you don't need to think about them any more than I'm thinking about the chair I'm sitting on right now or the keyboard beneath my fingers. But, if you've ever misplaced your glasses, you will know the feeling of desperation that sets in.

In that moment you can't think of *anything but* your glasses. Suddenly, the very thing you hardly ever noticed becomes the most important thing in the world.

Health, for most of us, works in a very similar way. We don't give it a second thought until we come down with a fever that keeps us in bed, or perhaps worse. This is because health is usually not an end in itself. We don't try to stay healthy for the sake of being healthy. We try to stay healthy so we can do more of the things we love and be there longer for the people we love. Thomas Fuller, the prolific historian and author, once remarked that "health is not valued till sickness comes." And he's right. Think about it. What happens as soon as you experience some form of sickness? You can't stop thinking about it. Have you ever tried to work through a massive headache? It's nearly impossible. What happens when you throw your back out? That twang of pain shooting through your body each time you stand up diverts your attention from whatever else you could have been thinking about. In the same way that people wear glasses to read, or I sit on this chair to write, our health serves as an essential means of accomplishing our goals.

Following the Law of Maintenance means that you will recognize the importance of attending to the three main pillars of bodily health: sleep, diet, and exercise. You will recognize that, if you violate the Law of Maintenance, you will eventually completely derail any chance you have for success because, like the desperation that sets in when you lose your glasses, the desperation that sets in when you lose your health will automatically siphon all your attention and energy away from your goals.

But, as you will recognize by now, one of the central themes of this book has been that, to maximize your success, you not only need to follow these laws; you need to learn to harness their power and make them work *for* you. When it comes to the Law of Maintenance, this means that you shouldn't just maintain your health so that you survive and avoid a major illness; rather, you should focus on becoming healthy so you can thrive.

We live in a world where the connection between the mind and body is not often recognized. Of course, we know that there is a connection of some kind. Our minds tell our bodies what to do, after all. But most of us don't recognize how close the connection is. Most of us don't recognize that our bodies also affect our minds, for example. But they do. Experts tell us that exercise increases the heart rate, which means that more oxygen gets pumped to the brain. This causes the release of hormones that encourage the growth of new brain cells and stimulate connections between existing cells. Exercise also helps to reduce stress hormones and give you more energy.

But exercise isn't the only way your body and brain are connected. They are also connected through diet. Did you know that the brain is the organ that takes the most energy of any organ in your body? It's true. Your brain needs fuel. And, just like with a car engine, the cleaner the fuel, the better. When you eat foods that have been processed or that contain refined sugars, you are causing your brain to function less efficiently. On the other hand, we know that people who eat healthier have more control over their emotions, have happier dispositions, and are able to focus better.

Finally, your body and brain are connected through sleep. Sleep is one of the most important components of success. Without the proper sleep, you will feel sluggish and your mental faculties will be clouded. What few people realize is that, when you're tired, one of the first things that your brain shuts down in order to conserve energy is your ability to resist temptation. You might have gone all week without eating junk food, but the day after you've had a terrible sleep you find yourself eating an entire box of rum chocolates. That, in turn, has a ripple effect that causes you to feel more tired, irritated, and unfocused.

The bottom line is simple: take care of your body if you want to maximize your success. Just like anything in life, your body needs proper maintenance in order to run properly for as long as possible. But don't fall into the trap of thinking that taking care of your health is all about not getting sick. It is that, but it's also much more. Taking care of your health is also about maximizing your performance.

So, take a little time to learn what your body needs and give it that. If you need ten hours of sleep every night to be at your best, get ten hours of sleep. If you need to eat one meal a day, do that. If you need to work out every day, do that. If you're better when you work out three times a week, then do that. Don't be afraid to experiment to figure out what your body needs. If you do, it will directly impact your success.

47. The Law of the Road Less Traveled

Two roads diverged in a wood, and I took the one less traveled by. And that has made all the difference.
—Robert Frost

The Law of the Road Less Traveled states that success requires you to take the path that is more difficult and lonelier than the one most people take.

There's an ancient Greek parable called *The Choice of Hercules*, in which Hercules, the son of Zeus, heads out one morning to run an errand for his father. As he was walking down the road, he began to think about how others he knew seemed to be enjoying a life of pleasure, while his life was filled with hard work. As he was thinking about this, he came upon a fork in the road. He stopped, uncertain which way to go. The road on his right was narrow, rough, and filled with hills, but far in the distance he could see the most breathtaking blue mountains. The road on his left was winding and smooth. He could see that it passed through a lush, green meadow, filled with countless flowers. It had large trees along the path that provided shade from the hot sun, and he could hear a choir of birds singing the most enchanting tune. But, if he looked past all this beauty, he could see, far in the distance, that the path led to a deep, foreboding fog.

As Hercules stood there, trying to decide which path to take, he saw two women walking toward him, one down each path. The woman coming from the smooth, pleasant path reached him first, and Hercules saw that she was very beautiful. When she spoke, her eyes sparkled and her words were comforting. She promised that if Hercules followed her, he would never have any troubles, and his life would be filled with every pleasure imaginable. This woman was called Pleasure.

When the woman from the other path reached him, she made a very different promise. She said that, if Hercules were to follow her, he would have such great difficulties that he would think about turning around with every single step he took. But, if he made it the whole way to the end of the path without giving up, he would reach the beautiful blue mountains and have endless fame. When Hercules asked this woman what her name was, she told him that people often call her Labor, but that she preferred to be called Virtue.

Hercules decided to take Virtue as his guide, so he put is hand in hers and set off down the difficult path. As a result, he lived a life of toil, hardship and suffering, while everyone else around him bathed in pleasure. But, because of his choice, only he has been immortalized as a hero throughout history, while the masses who took the path of pleasure have been long forgotten.

This famous story illustrates the struggle we all face between immediate gratification and long-term reward. We all know that very few things that are worth aiming at can be achieved easily. And we know that almost nothing worth having can be had quickly. Yet, we're hardwired to be motivated by immediate pleasure.

The road to success is always the road less traveled, which is also the road of delayed gratification. Success requires that you take it. There's no secret door or hidden path. It's there in plain sight, and everybody is faced with the same choice that Hercules faced. For most of us, taking the road less traveled will not require toil and hardship for our entire lives. But it will require that we put off immediate pleasure for future rewards. That's a guarantee.

Choosing the path of delayed gratification is not natural for most of us. Most of us would rather have what we want right now and deal with the consequences later. And that's why most people aren't successful. They go out with friends instead of staying home to work on their important project. They go through the drive-thru for lunch instead of getting up ten minutes earlier to make a salad before work. They watch a movie instead of reading a book. They choose a partner that makes them feel safe instead of one who challenges them to be a better person. They shirk responsibility instead of welcoming it. They play the victim instead of taking charge of the situation. They opt for the easy answer instead of carefully weighing opinions from all sides. They look for shortcuts instead of putting their head down and getting to work. In short, people who are unsuccessful take the road of pleasure, rather than the road of virtue. And this means they live lives that are not aligned with the Laws of Success.

I believe that we all know on some level that the road to success is the road of delayed gratification. But it's not an easy choice to make. This whole book is about helping you make the choice to walk the path of virtue every single day. My hope is that it will help you navigate the difficult terrain along that path just a little bit better. Because, if you're serious about having success in any area of your life, you *must* take the road less traveled.

Conclusion

You don't have to be great to start, but you have to start
to be great.

—Zig Ziglar

I would like to thank you for taking the time to read this
book. I hope that you have found it interesting and
inspiring. But most of all, I hope that you have found in
it some strategies and tactics that you can put into action
immediately. The time you've invested in this book will
have been a waste if you don't put anything you've learned
from it into practice. Remember these words of David
Viscott: "If you have the courage to begin, you have the
courage to succeed."

***

Having read through all forty-seven laws in this book, you
might feel a bit overwhelmed. In this conclusion, I want to
share with you one more law that I hope will help you apply
what you've read. This law could go by many different
names. It could be called the Law of the First Step or the Law
of the First Bite. Personally, I like to think about it as the

Law of Bird by Bird, based on the way Anne Lamott has described it in her bestselling book by that very name. Lamott tells us that her book, *Bird by Bird*, is inspired by a story about her father and brother. She explains that, as a child, her brother had put off doing a school project about birds for months. It was the day before the assignment was due and, as he sat there, overwhelmed by the amount of work he had to do in such a short amount of time, their father simply said, "Just take it bird by bird, buddy, bird by bird."

If you're feeling overwhelmed by everything in this book, I would encourage you with this same advice: just take it one law at a time. Pick the one law that strikes you as particularly useful for *you* and commit to following it for a week. Then, once you've begun to build up some momentum, try incorporating another law into your life. Once you've managed to observe both laws consistently, add another, and then another. As you continue to do this, you will find that your momentum increases as well. If you do this consistently, you *will* be successful—because you will be making incredible progress toward your ideal.

I wish you all the best on your journey to success!

***

If you have found this book helpful, or if you have any other constructive feedback, I would be grateful if you could take a few minutes to write an honest review on Amazon.

About the Author

Henry Bergen has more than a decade of experience as a productivity coach and consultant. As an expert strategist, he is committed to turning the latest cutting-edge research into actionable steps that help people improve their productivity, time management, and sense of fulfillment.

On his road to becoming a productivity expert, Henry earned a Ph.D. in ancient history, lived on a farm for three years, started four businesses, and traveled the world. Through these diverse experiences, he eventually began to notice a pattern: No matter the industry or area of life, the people who manage to turn their most ambitious dreams into reality all have the same mindset and engage in the same patterns of behavior.

Ever since this light bulb went on, he has been obsessed with developing this same mindset in his own life. Today he spends his time helping people transform their lives by learning to set ambitious goals, make realistic plans, and follow through by taking consistent action.

Printed in Great Britain
by Amazon